Love Letters

straight

From The Heart

Love Letters straight From The Heart

True Stories of Passion and Heartbreak

Nigel Williams

ROBSON BOOKS

First published in Great Britain in 2001 by Robson Books,
64 Brewery Road, London N7 9NT

A member of the Chrysalis Group

British Library Cataloguing in Publication Data
A catalogue record for this title is available from the British Library.

ISBN 1 86105 445 9

Typeset by SX composing DTP, Rayleigh, Essex
Printed by Creative Print & Design (Wales), Ebbw Vale

Dedicated to Estelle and Antonia, two girls who fill my
heart with love.

Acknowledgements

Many thanks to Paul Robinson for the introduction to 'Cuddle on the Couch'. Also Paul Chantler, Keith Pringle, Kevin Palmer, Jana Rangooni, Francis Currie, Jim Hicks, Phil Riley and Richard Huntingford for their support of Love Letters.

Introduction

Life as a radio DJ isn't all it's cracked up to be. For a start it's not a 'proper job' is it? Earning money for having a good time seems a little obscene really, especially when you consider how hard some people have to work to earn a crust. I've been the voice on the radio for eighteen years now: that's about twenty thousand hours in a studio alone with a microphone. You could say I've had plenty of time to contemplate my situation. Just as a listener sometimes wonders what it would be like to be in the studio, I would wonder about what was happening in the lives of my listeners. I remember asking myself if what I was doing really mattered to anyone; I knew that many people listened to the radio to help them through their daily routine, but did it really make a difference to their lives?

In 1989 I was given a Sunday evening 'Love Songs' show. At first it was the usual radio fare of romantic music and requests from listeners. Initially, I found the show really hard to present because I had always hated that cheesy sound that was associated with 'Love' shows; I wanted to sound real. After a while I began to relax and for the first time in my career, I was Nigel the soft-hearted guy who just happened to be on the radio, not Nigel the DJ.

One evening I opened a letter from a woman called Jennifer who was on the verge of breaking up with her husband. Over several handwritten pages, she told her story from the day they first met. It seemed that the marriage had become bogged down with petty arguments and they had lost sight of the magic that brought them together. The letter was so emotional, I decided to break the radio station's policy of 'more music, less talk' and read the whole letter on the air. Within a few days, I received another letter from Jennifer. She told me that when her husband heard me read out their story, he had burst into tears and vowed to try and sort out their problems. As far as Jennifer was concerned, I had saved their marriage. I knew I had been 'saved' too. I now knew that the work I was doing was important and that I could make a difference to people's lives.

Over the years, the stories have continued to arrive and now I find myself introducing my first book based on those original letters. The following pages contain many touching, romantic and sometimes titillating situations. They display the amazing variety of things that human nature can make us do in the pursuit of love. Some of the stories will make you laugh and some will make you cry. One thing is certain and that is that they will make you think about your own relationship. You may become a better lover as a result!

I would like to send out a huge thank you to everyone who has written to me over the years. I have tried to contact all the contributors of the stories contained in this book, but unfortunately (although understandably) some were sent in anonymously. If this applies to you, I would love to hear from you.

Oh, by the way, I couldn't allow my listeners' intimate affairs to be published without baring all myself. See if you can guess which one is my story.

Love

Nigel Williams

Write to me c/o Robson Books
e-mail :loveletters@njwilliams.com
or visit www.njwilliams.com

Karen and Doug

It's Not Just the Uniform . . .

Phil and I had been living together for over six years. I'd got used to all of his idiosyncrasies and I thought nothing could surprise me. One day, we'd just finished our dinner when Phil suddenly announced that he had been seeing someone else and it was all over between us. The shock was made even worse by the cold and matter of fact way he delivered his message.

I was devastated, I had no idea this was going on. I had trusted him and now he had made a complete fool of me. Fortunately, the rest of the split was quicker. We agreed to a fifty–fifty split and I moved out of the house as quickly as possible. I also decided that I wasn't going to sit around and mope. I was going to get out and about and catch up with all those people I'd neglected over the years. I acted so fast I didn't even get to spend one night in my new flat, I booked a flight to California to go and see my cousins.

It was just the therapy I needed. I had a great time with my cousins Janet and Burt; we went to Yosemite National Park and then on to Reno Nevada to visit Janet's daughter and her husband. I was really looking forward to it because I'd never met Patsy and Gene.

Two years ago cousin Janet was diagnosed with breast cancer. Fortunately she was successfully treated. Ever since then, the whole family had become involved with fund-raising for cancer charities. During my visit, they were organising a sponsored twenty-four hour charity walk and they asked me if I wanted to join in. There was a really great atmosphere there; it was almost as if the whole town had turned out. Some were in fancy dress, some were singing songs and some had brought enough food for a trip to Antarctica rather than a few laps round the athletics track.

Gene worked for the local fire department and every year he always organised a big team for the walk. Gene introduced me to some of his colleagues and before you knew it, I was surrounded by a sea of sexy uniforms! One of them in particular seemed really nice; his name was Doug. Cousin Patsy could see we were obviously hitting it off, so made herself scarce and arranged a later lift home for me. Suddenly everyone seemed to disappear and I was left alone with Doug. We seemed to have so much in common, it was really strange. Pity I'm going home in a couple of days, I thought to myself, I could really enjoy myself with Doug.

The next day Cousin Patsy was bursting to find out what happened. She told me that Doug was normally really shy around women and he never went out on dates. Our girls' gossip was suddenly interrupted by the phone ringing. Patsy tipped me a wink as she handed me the receiver. Doug's voice boomed down the earpiece as he confidently asked me out to dinner. If he's the shy type, he's certainly covering it up well, I thought.

Our first dinner date was an efficient affair, but afterwards we took a walk around the marina and back to his house. The formality of the restaurant had stifled our conversation. Now, in the freedom of the open air, I could feel the sexual chemistry building between us. What's the point, my head was screaming, you're going home in a couple of days.

At the end of my holiday, Doug offered me his e-mail address and promised to keep in touch. I couldn't wait to get back to work in London, just to see if he'd left a message. Among the endless list of office junk e-mails, Doug's message stood out of the screen. As I read, he explained that he had feelings for me, but didn't know what to do as I left so soon. I quickly replied, saying I felt the same way too. But what were we going to do about it?

Over the next few months, we exchanged e-mails and revealed more about ourselves than we ever would have in person. We decided I should go back to America for three weeks in September and give things a try. That's when our true romance really started, though it came as no surprise to me because after all those heart-searching e-mails, I knew I had fallen in love with Doug on my computer. The irony of the situation struck me. I had been so betrayed by Phil, at the time, I was sure I could never love again. Now here I was, totally trusting a man who was thousands of miles away!

Doug was supposed to visit England for Christmas, but I thought that it was not a good time to come to London; it's not cold and it never snows. Doug had been telling me about his 'winter wonderland' that was right outside his window. The next thing I knew, I was sitting at the table and preparing myself for my first Christmas dinner of pheasant and pumpkin pie.

Doug had been at work at the fire department throughout the night. It was the best Christmas present ever to pick him up from the fire station in the morning. He'd been up half the night fighting a house fire and looked exhausted, but sweetly presented me with the beautiful gift box containing a spectacular bracelet. My surprise for Doug was a little different. It was the ski season and I had told Doug that I had never tried it. He told me I didn't know what I was missing and promised to give me a lesson right there and then. When we got on the piste, Doug started off on his beginner's lesson. I listened intently as he showed me how to make a 'snow plough'. Then came the moment of truth when he told me to start moving. Suddenly, I just shot off down the slope, perfectly in control, showing off the lessons I had secretly taken in England before I came. I'm not sure if it counted as a Christmas present for Doug, but it certainly gave him a shock.

The holidays just flew by. On New Year's Eve, Doug took me to a posh party at his colleague's house. They had a balcony overlooking the city of Reno and at the stroke of midnight, Doug and I stood out there watching the fireworks over the city. At that moment, I knew I would remember this feeling forever; I wanted to be with Doug for the rest of my life.

The problem was, despite being our closest ally, America couldn't offer me a visa to go and work out there unless I had some special skill like being a doctor or a scientist. I knew that this situation was holding Doug back from fully committing himself to me, and it was hurting so much because my heart longed to hear Doug confirm that he felt the same way. I wasn't going to give up that easily. Not only did I learn to ski, but while I was there I got myself a job in the local ski resort in charge of guest services. Not the best job in the world, but they could get me a temporary working visa.

So Nigel, I am off on Monday and who knows when I'm coming back. I really have a good feeling about our future together in America, I hope my instincts prove right . . .

Let's hope Doug pops the question before it's too late, eh?

2

Dawson and Kate

My Flight of Fantasy

It was eleven years ago and I was on a flight to Los Angeles. This wasn't just business or a holiday; I was on my way to live in LA for good. My sister had convinced me that I stood a better chance with my construction business in the USA, so I was on my way.

Everyone on the flight was asleep except my three-year-old niece. I awoke with a start to find her gone from her seat. The adrenalin kicked in and I scurried around the aircraft in a small panic. There weren't that many places to look and eventually I found her in the cockpit, sitting on the lap of the co-pilot. I am ashamed to say I was speechless at seeing a woman in control of the aircraft and she must have realised it because my jaw practically hit the cabin floor. Kate cracked a few jokes about my niece flying the aeroplane and I relaxed. In the end, we talked for a good couple of hours. By the end of the conversation, we had arranged to meet up at her hotel in LA.

With our feet on solid ground, we continued to hit it off in a manner I had never experienced before. Kate and I met whenever she was on a stopover or when I was on business in London. After a year of this I knew Kate was the woman for me. I decided I was going to pop the question, but wanted it to be the perfect romantic moment. I froze her engagement ring in an ice cube and slipped it into her glass of Coke, but because of the dark liquid she didn't see it and nearly swallowed it. I grabbed the drink from her and ruined her favourite sweater in the process. The next attempt was a jack-in-the-box. On the lid I wrote my proposition and put the ring on the jack's hand. When it burst open, it nearly gave her a heart attack and she began to hit me with the box before bursting into tears and accepting my offer. A fairytale wedding followed a year later in LA.

Now it seemed as if my life was perfect. My business was more successful than I ever imagined and I used my construction skills to build Kate the house of her dreams, which she called her 'Little White Palace'.

We really wanted children. Kate had a plan to enjoy her career first, then to retire to look after kids.

After seven years we were still childless but then disaster struck. Kate was involved in an air accident that left her in a coma for two weeks. She did wake up, but she was paralysed from the waist down. Amazingly her doctor in intensive care was a researcher into paralysis and offered an experimental operation and treatment. The seventeen-hour operation miraculously worked, but it was still a long road to recovery. Kate had to learn how to walk all over again. It was a testing time, full of tears and arguments but in the end, it brought us even closer.

Kate's flying days were obviously over. We decided it was 'now or never' for children, so we tried – and tried. Eventually we tried IVF six times, which resulted in three painful miscarriages. Kate and I grew further apart and often argued in public and stormed out on each other at home. I even hit her once, which I'm terribly ashamed of. This had to be the end. I filed for divorce but Kate refused to sign the documents. We decided to go for counselling, which helped us a lot and we agreed to try adoption, but we were turned down everywhere because of our marital problems.

We weren't going to give up on our quest for children. We found a surrogate mother, a young girl who needed some money, but she took the money and ran.

Surely our lives couldn't get any worse at this point, but they did. A stranger came into our home posing as a repair man and raped Kate in the basement. He was a serial rapist who had killed four women, but thankfully our local security guards came to check on this so-called repair man and caught him. Poor Kate might have escaped with her life, but she was emotionally scarred. She was once the life and soul of any party, but now she retreated from her social life altogether. She was so scared of entering the basement that I had it converted into an indoor swimming pool but she still never goes down there alone.

I was beginning to think there was nothing I could do to put a smile back on my wife's face. I decided to do something extravagant and romantic. I filled our entire house with silvery balloons and a carpet of rose petals all the way to the bedroom. When Kate came home from shopping, she fell into my arms and we made love all night. It was a magical experience, we felt so special, as if no one could harm us. Just for one night we left all our troubles outside the bedroom door.

Our night of loving wasn't just magical, it was a miracle because that was the night we made twins! I can't tell you how proud and excited I was when little Joshua and Bonnie were born.

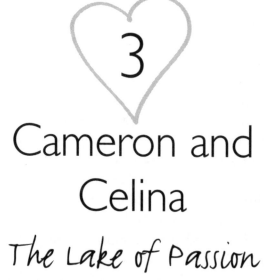

3

Cameron and Celina

The Lake of Passion

For the first eighteen years of my life, I barely met a girl, let alone had a girlfriend. This was mainly due to the fact that I went to an all-boys' school and I was too busy thinking about my studies to contemplate the opposite sex.

At the end of my final year at school, I managed to achieve the grades I needed to go on to university, but it was all becoming a bit too strenuous, so I decided to take a gap year. I wanted to travel to America on my own rather than with a friend, so I would be able to spend quite a bit of time with family who lived there.

My first stop was California where some of my cousins lived. I would end up staying with them for two weeks. Little did I know that those two weeks would change my life for ever.

One night, my cousins, Laura and Anna, who were both the same age as me, were invited to a friend's party. They took me along so they could show off their cousin's 'adorable accent'. That was when I first met Celina. To say she was an angel would have been an understatement. She was simply stunning! After talking long into the night, Celina and I decided we would meet up the next day down at the local lake where she worked. She told me she got free use of a jet ski and we could go out on the lake together. This one-off day out ended up becoming a daily trip for the remaining few days I had left in California.

On the last day I was out on the lake with Celina as usual. She pulled the jet ski into a secluded cove and suddenly threw me off the back. As I protested and shouted obscenities, she came in after me and before I could say another word, planted her luscious lips on mine. The next thing I knew she was slipping off her swimming costume and gesturing that I should take her right there and then in the lake. It was so sexy! I didn't care if anyone could see.

The next day came all too soon and I had a plane to catch. Cousin Laura and Anna accompanied me to the airport, along with Celina clutching my arm, begging me to stay. Just before boarding at the gate, I gave Celina my home and e-mail address and phone number. With that I gave her a single red rose with a note attached reading, 'Words simply cannot express the love I have for you in my heart. I will always love you no matter what.'

Months later, I was back in London. Celina wrote or phoned regularly at first, but as time went by, we became more interested in things closer to home. I was starting university soon and had to begin planning my future. Celina was busy preparing herself for a new job and, gradually, we lost touch.

Two years later I was in the middle of my studies and wrapped up in my own little world. Suddenly there was a knock at the door of my apartment. I opened the door to the biggest surprise I'd ever had. Celina was standing there with that unmistakable soft smile upon her face.

Since that moment, our love has been nothing short of a fairytale and we haven't looked back. We are so in love with each other that we are getting married as soon as we can. We have been living together for nearly two years now and to add to all of that, our first child is on the way. I have so much to look forward to, but mostly I am looking forward to spending the rest of my life with the woman I love and my soon-to-be-born son or daughter.

4

Brian and Lorna

A Question of Aura

When I met Lorna we were both in very similar circumstances. Both of us were going through painful divorces and both of us had kids. Having so much in common brought us closer together and our friendship quickly grew into love.

We were both carrying a lot of emotional baggage and, during the early days, living together was difficult. I remember once packing my suitcase and just running away to the remotest place I could think of just to get my life into perspective. I was sitting in the middle of nowhere thinking what an idiot I was when I caught sight of a figure in the distance making a beeline for me. Pretty soon, it became clear that it was Lorna. She just held out her hands and said, 'Come here Brian'. I couldn't begin to work out how on earth she had found me. When I asked her, she just said, 'When you love somebody this much, you don't need maps or signs – I just followed your aura.' After that, my love for her was set in the foundations of my heart.

Lorna wanted more kids. I had my reservations at first, but agreed after a while and we had two wonderful boys. After that, I decided it was time for the snip. We now had five kids between us and I thought that was enough. But it wasn't enough for Lorna and as the boys grew up, she longed for another little baby to care for. I just couldn't agree to reversing my vasectomy. I just hoped she would understand eventually.

My kids from my first marriage were living with their mother. One day my ex-wife called me and told me she was having a lot of trouble with our son and persuaded me that living with Lorna and me might do him some good. It soon became clear that he had some serious emotional problems and his behaviour drove Lorna up the wall. At the time I didn't know how bad things were. But she took solace in the arms of an old friend and got herself pregnant. I was heartbroken, but I still loved her. Lorna told me she was going to have an abortion, but knowing how much she wanted another baby, I knew it was going to be a terrible ordeal for her so I said that I would stand by her if she wanted to keep the baby.

I knew I was going to have to move my son back to his mother's if I was going to save our relationship. After that I gave her lots more space to breathe and it seemed to work. She was much happier and our sex life turned extra passionate. Finally, I began to relax.

It was Monday 27 July when I returned from work to find no car in the drive and the house in darkness. Immediately the hairs stood up on the back of my neck; something was very wrong. I opened the door to find the house stripped bare. At first I thought it was burglars, but then I found a note from Lorna, telling me she was sorry, but she had gone to live with 'Jerry' and taken the kids with her. I had no idea who Jerry was or that Lorna was even having an affair. It suddenly dawned on me that all that passion we had been experiencing in bed was for him and not me.

I still think of Lorna every night and wonder if there was anything I could have done to keep her. Was it the fact that I was no longer potent that put her off? I still don't know how she found me when I ran away all those years ago. If she truly can sense my aura, she will know how heartbroken I am.

5

Elaine and Rob

A Holiday Romance with a Difference

I'd been seeing this guy from work on and off for five years. Chris was still officially married with a couple of kids. They'd split up before I really got involved but Chris had never really let go. All my friends had been telling me for ages that he was just using me, but I didn't listen. He spun me all sorts of lies about commitment as the years went by, but he never really meant any of them.

One day I woke up and thought, 'What am I doing with my life? I'm thirty-five and acting like a love-struck teenager.' I decided that was it, I was going to dump Chris and all his pathetic excuses and find myself someone new. But how was I going to do it? I'd tried to leave Chris a hundred times before, but he always turned on the charm and made me more promises. I needed a plan.

I decided to take some holiday leave from work at short notice. At least this would get me out of temptation's way. As I scanned through the holiday bargains on the TV text pages, I was already beginning to feel a sense of escape. In the end, I never called Chris to tell him it was over, I thought I'd just leave him not knowing what was going on, like he'd left me so many times before.

But where should I go? I'd never been travelling by myself before. Just then, on the TV, 'Cyprus – special Flight Only bargain' flashed up on the screen. Before I knew what I was doing, I was on the phone, credit card in hand, booking the flight.

I arrived at the airport with no idea where I was going to stay, and stood in a huge queue for taxis (I remember it well because I was dying for the loo). I asked a friendly looking guy behind me to keep my place and look after my bags. When I returned he started chatting me up, which was the last thing I needed! I tolerated it for a while, after all, he had done me a favour. His name was Rob and he seemed really knowledgeable about Cyprus.

'I lived here as a kid,' he explained. 'My dad was in

the Forces.' He asked me where I was staying. I wanted to tell him that I had it all sorted but he could tell from my lack of answer that I had no idea. 'Don't worry, I know someone who will fix you up with a great place – wanna share a cab?' By now, I had no choice and I wondered what I was letting myself in for. The taxi drove along the dusty roads and took us to this beautiful spot, miles away from all the hustle and bustle.

The woman who owned the apartments greeted Rob with a real hug, like they were long-lost friends. I was intrigued. I was shown up into a wonderful room overlooking the sea. It was so perfect, better than I had imagined. This was going to be a real escape from Chris and his lies. I was so tired. The balmy atmosphere and the tranquillity were working their magic and I fell asleep.

I was woken by a loud knock at the door. 'Elaine, it's Rob – do you fancy a swim?' My eyes sprang open, it was dark and I couldn't remember where I was. Slowly the last few hours came back to me.

'It's dark,' I shouted, wishing he would just go away.

'Dark is best, trust me. Let's go,' he insisted, 'you'll miss it!' Eventually, I went along with it; anything for a quiet life. I was going to do this one thing and then tell him to leave me alone.

Rob led me down to the beach. At first I could see nothing and I began to get scared. Here I was with a perfect stranger in the middle of nowhere, anything could happen. But something told me it would be all right. As we arrived on the beach, my eyes began to adjust to the dark. 'Look up,' said Rob. There was no moon that night, just an amazing blanket of stars; I had never seen anything like it. The warmth of the evening air seemed to warm my soul, and I began to question why I was so distrustful of Rob. After all, judging by the hug he got from the owner of the apartments, he couldn't be all that bad.

Lights winked at us from ships on the horizon as we gazed out to sea. Everything seemed so quiet and still. Now I knew this was going to be a moment I would remember for ever. I finally began to relax. Rob pulled out a bottle of wine from his rucksack and we sat and talked. It all seemed so easy. He was the first man I'd ever spoken to who seemed to be really in touch with his own feelings. I ended up telling him all about my past and he seemed to understand what I was talking about.

'Stuff happens,' he said. 'I think you need to have a lot of forgiveness in you. Life's a lot easier then and you'd be surprised what the benefits are.' We sat on the beach for what must've been hours. Rob made me feel that I was in control of what happened next. Now this is going to sound corny and it wasn't the wine! I just wanted to kiss this guy for restoring my faith in men. So I did! I was on holiday, sitting on a beach under the stars and enjoying a bottle of wine. I could do whatever I wanted.

The next morning I woke up and realised what I'd done. What about this woman who runs the apartments, maybe there's something going on?

Am I setting myself up to be the mistress again? When I saw Rob, I was decidedly cold towards him. We had breakfast together and he was just beaming. Just then the owner of the apartments came out, giving Rob a huge knowing smile. She looked very tanned, slim and attractive. She put her arm around him and gave him a big hug. I began to feel my blood boil. I waited until she was out of earshot and snapped at him, 'I don't know how you've got the cheek to do that in front of me.'

Rob just smiled and then began to laugh uncontrollably. That just made me angrier. 'I'm sorry, I should have told you when I brought you here – that's my half-sister. I would have told you earlier but you might have thought that I was just recommending this place because I was related to her.' If that wasn't enough of an explanation, there was more. 'Remember I told you about the need for forgiveness – well, my dad had an affair when I was just a kid, and she's the product of that relationship – I love her to bits.' What could I say? After that I found a trust for Rob that I didn't know I possessed. We spent the next two weeks in fantasyland.

Now it's years later, Rob and I still see each other, but only as friends. I have never forgotten the magic of that holiday and how it gave me a new outlook on life. These days I am so much happier. I still haven't found Mr Right but I think I know a lot more about how to look.

6

Mandy and Steven

'Don't Look at My Passport Photograph . . .'

I couldn't believe my luck when the man with the piercing blue eyes flashed a smile back at me. Usually I wasn't very lucky in love for various reasons. Steven was absolutely incredible to look at. His blond hair and tanned skin made him look like a lifeguard or something. He was very tall, but this suited me down to the ground because I am six feet tall myself. Luckily Steven and I hit it off and so began our adventure. I had no idea how far we were going to go.

Steven and I had romantic dinners for two, went away for steamy, sexy weekends in the country and had lots of cosy nights in. Not only was the sex brilliant, but so was the rest of life with Steven; he really was one in a million. Things were getting very serious between us and I could not stand being without him. Every time he left, I imagined he was walking out of my life and I would never see him again. I asked Steven to move in with me and, to my surprise, he agreed. Now I had everything I wanted, my life was complete.

Steven kept asking me to go abroad with him for a romantic holiday. I kept on turning him down because I didn't want him to see my passport. I just told him I was scared of flying and he seemed to accept that. One night, Steven and I went out for another romantic dinner, but this was no ordinary romantic night out. All of a sudden, Steven dropped down on to one knee and proposed. This was such a terrific moment and I should have been over the moon, but instead I just burst into tears. Poor Steven just didn't know what to think. I told him we really needed to talk.

The journey home seemed to take for ever, part of me was glad of the traffic because it was delaying the inevitable. I was going to have to tell Steven about my dark secret. My stomach was turning as we pulled up to the house. I knew that once I had told Steven my secret, he would be out of my life for ever. He kept saying, 'I don't care what you're going to tell me, I want us to be together for ever.' I could see my whole world crumbling as he sat me down and started caressing my face.

I stared into those beautiful eyes and trembling, I said, 'Steven, I can't marry you because five years ago, I was a man, but now, through the wonders of medicine I'm a woman and I'll always love you.' At first he just told me not to be stupid but as I explained what it was like to be transsexual, I saw him begin to comprehend the truth. I saw the pain in his eyes building. Suddenly he got up and walked out of the house without saying a word.

By the time four weeks had passed, I knew Steven was like all the other men who had gone before him. Once they found out the truth, they ran a mile. I felt so lonely; I sat and stared at Steven's belongings, which he was obviously too scared to come and pick up. I took one of his sweaters and held it close to me. The faint smell of his cologne comforted me a little and I fell asleep on the sofa.

Later that evening, I was shocked into consciousness by the doorbell. I'd been asleep for hours and it was nearly midnight. I opened the door to find Steven standing there. I beckoned him inside without saying a word and directed him to his stuff. But Steven didn't follow, he stood in the doorway and said, 'I know it's been a long time but I had to think it over. Mandy, I fell in love with you, not your past.' He outstretched his arms, 'If you'll take me back, I'd like to start all over again.'

We did a lot of talking after that, and we're now

happier than ever. Unfortunately, we could never get married in England, because in the eyes of the law, I'm still a man. However, we did have our own little ceremony with close friends and family, which was good enough for us.

7

Alan and Claire

Alan's Dangerous Dance

I was at a farewell party for one of my friends. She was going off to work in the Middle East and a huge crowd had turned up to wish her well. I didn't know many of the people there and, I have to be honest, I was feeling pretty unsociable. Aged thirty-four, I was yet to find my soulmate in life and on this particular night, I couldn't be bothered to continue my search. I just stood in the corner and spoke to a few guys I knew and that was it.

Later in the evening, some people were trying to get the dancing going. One of them was a woman I'd never met before. She walked straight up to me and said, 'Don't tell me you're not dancing – with a bum like that.' I was stunned slightly by her boldness. She stood with her arm outstretched and with that she led me on to the dance floor. It was an extraordinary meeting, but Claire was an extraordinary person. This was the start of a relationship full of passion and laughter.

Everything in my life suddenly felt like it was falling into place. In fact, things with Claire took off so quickly that I moved in with her only six weeks after I met her. 'So this is the love everyone is always talking about,' I thought. Claire and I were so happy when we were together; we devoted so much of our time to each other that we lost contact with a lot of our friends. We were so committed to our future, we started up a joint bank account, bought a car together and even started to plan our wedding. We actually had names for our unborn children.

But there was no middle ground with Claire. She either loved someone or something or she hated them or it. Fortunately she loved me – for now. Things started to change when I got a new job, which took up a bit more of my time. There was a lot more money coming in and we needed it because we both had some ugly debts. Claire began to develop a jealousy complex. If I came home any more than ten minutes later than planned, I would be subjected to endless questions. I tried my best to be patient and attempted to answer all of her (sometimes ridiculous) questions. As time went by, her tantrums became more outrageous. I was accused of having affairs, the lot; I really don't know what started it all. It got so bad that I was accused of fancying her younger sister, right in front of her whole family. I tried so hard to assure her that I was committed to our relationship, but the more I comforted her, the worse it got. Eventually I just snapped, I took a few of my things, bundled them into the car, and left.

I didn't speak to Claire for two weeks. I knew I still loved her, so I decided to call to see how she was. She seemed to have cooled off a bit but certainly wasn't full of remorse. We agreed to meet on neutral ground to talk things over. I drove to a pub she had suggested and waited for half an hour, but there was still no sign of Claire. I phoned her at home, there was no answer. Finally, I gave up and walked out to the car park, only to discover someone had stolen my car. I went back into the pub to call the police, but then the penny dropped. The whole meeting had just been Claire's plan to get the car off me. She had obviously brought the spare keys and driven off while I was waiting inside. I was more hurt than angry. What had I done to make someone I love hate me so much?

I decided to let it all go and started my life all over again. A few months later, I received a letter from Claire saying that she was so sorry and begging me to go back to her. She said it was all her fault and nothing to do with me, but didn't really explain where all the jealousy was coming from.

I know that I love Claire, but I don't know what to do. If I go back, what happens if it all blows up again? I don't know if I could stand the pain and confusion for a second time. What would you do?

8

Marilyn and George

I've Got a Secret and I've Just Got to Tell Someone

If anyone had asked me to describe the perfect man back when I was still a teenager at school, I would have described a dark and dangerous-looking man. Someone who was sensitive but strong and . . . a doctor! Well, years later my dream came true. I met Dr Simon and over six and a half years we had fallen in love and planned to marry.

It was my birthday. Simon had told me that he had special plans for us that evening once his hospital shift was over. I had been telling my colleague George about it all day, in fact I was sure he was fed up with hearing about my fairytale relationship with Simon. But he was so nice; he never said a word.

George and I were just packing up for the day when Simon called. He had that sound in his voice, which prepared me for what was about to come. 'Marilyn, I'm so sorry, Dr Harris has called in sick so I've got to work the night shift.' This is the sort of thing you have to get used to when you're dating a doctor. But I couldn't hide the disappointment from my face; after all this was *my* day! The next thing I knew George came to the rescue and offered to take me out instead. It didn't seem like he was threatening my relationship, I just thought he was being sweet.

In the restaurant I just burst into tears. I had been looking forward to my birthday dinner with Simon for so long. But George was there to comfort me; his arms were so warm and welcoming and the kiss that followed just seemed so natural. It may sound strange, but I didn't even notice that I was doing something wrong. I obviously had feelings for George and hadn't realised it. The kiss triggered an explosion of love in my heart and before you knew it, I was in his bedroom, making sure he felt the full force of it.

Now I was trapped! I was so in love with George in a way that I never knew was possible. I couldn't believe that I was cheating on Simon, the man whom I had loved for so long. The man I was going to marry in a few months time! Yet, I couldn't pull myself away from

George. Then the worst thing that could happen at that time, happened. Just two months before the wedding, I found out I was pregnant. There was no doubt in my mind that it was George's baby. I just didn't know who to tell, so I told Simon that it was his baby.

The wedding went ahead that summer and it was one of the most happy, but confusing times of my life. The absolute love that I had always felt for Simon was confirmed and everything was going so perfectly. But I kept thinking of George. At first, my solution had seemed so simple, but now I was feeling the guilt of not telling the true father. Not to mention the way I had lied to my husband. I remembered the way his entire face lit up with joy when I told him we were going to start a family. It was overwhelming, I knew in my heart that I could never tell him that it was not his child.

George came to our wedding and he wished us a polite congratulations. We had talked before and he understood that we could not be. At the wedding he seemed composed but at the reception, I noticed he was drinking a lot. Afterwards Simon and I jetted off on honeymoon to Bali and I tried to forget all about George.

Three weeks after we got back, I was catching up with my family and getting all the gossip from the wedding when someone said, 'It's such a shame about that George isn't it?' I went cold. What did they mean?

None of my family knew who George was and none of my friends knew the extent of my friendship with him, so nobody had told me that after the wedding, George had tried to drive home drunk and had a very bad accident. He was now in a coma.

I felt like I wanted to rush to George's bedside and stay there until he woke up, but I couldn't; people would want to know why. Now the feelings of guilt were getting worse. I would be lying in bed with my husband, but thinking of George every time I felt his baby kick. I knew that I must tell him the truth. In desperation, I secretly called George's flatmate to arrange to visit. Phil spoke softly and calmly explained that George had died four days ago. I cannot even begin to describe the utter pain that just stabbed through my entire body. The tears ran uncontrollably down my face. I just fell to the floor and felt as though I couldn't move. That evening I had to try to explain to my husband why I was still lying sobbing on the floor. I was trapped into this lie and I could never get out of it. Now that George was gone, I could never tell Simon because then I would lose everything.

I fell into a deep depression and I stopped eating. As a consequence of this I had a miscarriage. I am still not sure if this was for better or worse. The loss deepened my pain but it felt like a relief. I had lost the only part of George that I could ever have, but at the same time now I was completely free to start again with Simon.

I got better from my depression even though I could never tell anyone what had caused it, not even the doctors because I was afraid that Simon would find out. Six years on I still haven't forgotten about George. Simon's work takes him abroad a lot these days, so it gives me a lot of time to think. I know that a relationship should be built on trust and honesty but this lie has just gone too far and I can't tell Simon now. I pray that he never finds out, that nobody ever will.

I have found it a really huge help just to have written things down and got it all off my chest finally. I can't believe that I have just told you my secret. In a way it feels strange, but in a good way.

Penny and Terry

Out of the Frying Pan . . .

Four years ago, I was breathing a sigh of relief after finally escaping from a very violent relationship. Finally I was free to do anything, to see whoever I wanted, whenever I wanted. After all I had been through over the years, I was in no hurry to meet someone new.

I'm still not quite sure how it happened, but all of a sudden I was dating this guy called Terry. To tell you the truth, sometimes I was quite angry with myself for starting a relationship when I obviously wasn't ready. My common sense told me to end it, or at least not to get in too deep. But there must have been another side of me with different needs because the next thing I knew I was in bed with Terry, telling him that I loved him. He told me that he loved me too and that he wanted to move in with me. So, in the space of a few weeks I had got the old man out and a new man in.

My whirlwind romance with Terry continued and it was so wonderful, I told myself not to worry about being on the rebound and to get on with enjoying my life. After all I'd been through, I felt like I deserved it. We were married on 1 July, five months after we first met.

Most married couples wait at least a couple of months before having their first argument. We had ours on our wedding night. I don't even remember what started it but it became so heated that instead of consummating the marriage, I stormed out of the bridal suite and went home for the night. So much for the happiest day of my life! We made up, of course, and within a few months I was pregnant. The rows were still happening, it almost seemed as if the marriage sparked them off.

Terry and I were determined to do something to stop us arguing. We both thought a change of scenery would do us good, so we moved to Southend. It was supposed to be the start of a new life together, but nothing really changed. Eventually Terry made me so miserable, I went out on my own, got drunk and slept with someone else, just to get back at Terry. When I told him, he just went berserk. He went much further than I'd bargained for and that's when he hit me. I was eight months' pregnant at the time. The thought that Terry could harm the baby made me feel so angry that I grabbed a knife and lunged at him. 'Do it! I deserve it!' Terry shouted. I just dropped the knife and ran upstairs in floods of tears.

The following few months were quiet. Little Danny was born and everything went smoothly. As soon as the excitement over his arrival died down, the rows returned. This time they were worse than ever. We were at each other's throats one minute and making love the next. Consequently, it wasn't long before I was pregnant again. There were a lot of complications with this pregnancy, so I had to spend some time in hospital. I had taken in a teenage foster daughter a few months previous to this and she really helped out with things back at the house. One day she came in to see me and she was crying. At first she wouldn't tell me what it was all about, but I persisted and she told me that Terry had asked her for sex. The thought of Terry getting all horny around this sweet child made me feel nauseous and I just flew into a boiling rage. Who was I married to? Some pervert?

My patience was almost at an end but it took one more thing to finally do it for me. After little Ryan was born, Terry went out drinking and spent all our money. I was livid. How was I going to buy nappies and food for the baby? Terry responded by giving me a good kicking and went back out on the booze. I could take it no more, I went straight to the police and they put me in a women's refuge.

So that was that. The end of violent relationship, number two. Looking back, it seems like I jumped out of the frying pan and into the fire; I wish I had taken time to heal the wounds of my first relationship before finding someone new. I also think I should have been able to sense the warning signs that Terry was an abuser too. Right now, I do feel so lonely, but it's better this way. Maybe one day I will meet a man who can love me tenderly. Until then, it's just me and the kids.

Susan and Dave

Too Much Too Soon

It all began when I was just fifteen years old. Dave was my first love. If I had been a normal teenager it probably would have lasted for six months to a year and then one of us would have found somebody else. But not us, we went all the way, we got married! I was just eighteen at the time and I thought I was the luckiest woman in the world because I had done it before all my friends.

Looking back now, I can see that we were both still growing up in the early years of our marriage and I suppose that's why, when I met Andrew, I felt compelled to go with him. Andrew promised the world, it seemed so much more interesting than the daily routine of being married to Dave, and so I left.

Over the years Andrew and I had three children together, but of course life with Andrew turned out to be a lot less than he was promising. In fact it was just as mundane, if not worse, than life with Dave. My second marriage ended in divorce after twelve years.

I decided I should spend a while on my own, but I couldn't resist George. He was so kind to me and seemed so genuine. We had some spectacular nights out and I got some spectacular hangovers to match. This was a lot of fun to start with, but after a time I began to realise he couldn't do anything without the inclusion of alcohol. When I mentioned it to George, he told me not to be so silly.

It wasn't much longer before the abuse started. Sometimes George would just shout and call me names, but then physical abuse started and I knew I had to end it. But how was I to get away from him? I was so scared of what he would do when I tried to leave that I kept putting it off.

One day George and I had a huge row. It was getting so heated, I was just wishing I had thought out an escape plan. I was so sure that this time I was in for a real beating when suddenly he just stormed out of the house and never came back. The next day, I was thinking to myself, 'That turned out easier than I expected,' when suddenly the doorbell went and it was the police telling me that George had taken his own life. I felt totally drained inside and went through every emotion from grief to anger. It seemed as if nothing could go right for me. I couldn't even leave an abusive partner properly. I gradually sank into depression and wallowed in my own cesspool of emotions.

One morning I was sitting staring at the newspaper. It had been open at the same page for ages. I had been paralysed by my indifference for what seemed like hours. Suddenly my eyes focused on the agony column. I don't know why, but I picked up a pen and paper and poured out all my feelings about my life to the agony aunt. I never really expected a reply but actually she wrote back. She told me there was a light at the end of the tunnel and to hang on in there. 'How does she know that?' I thought.

The next day the phone was ringing and it was my stepdaughter telling me that my first husband Dave wanted to see me. What had I done? Why would he want to see me? I had nothing to give him. The more I thought about him, the more curious I became. I had to go.

The last time I saw Dave's face, it was streaming with tears as I was breaking his heart all those years ago. It was a face that still haunted me in my dreams and left me with a deep feeling of guilt.

As I waited in the café for Dave to arrive, my stomach was in knots. But as soon as he arrived, we just picked up where we left off. I felt like a teenager again. Two months later Dave asked if we could try again.

Dave and I have been truly happy for the past two years now; this time, I know in my heart we will always be together. You could say we were fated to be together, but then why did I have to go through all that to come full circle? Maybe I just met my perfect love too early.

Please tell Dave I love him with all my heart.

11

Dianne's Story

My First Real Love

I had fallen madly and deeply in love with a guy called Mark. He was the man I had been saving myself for. All of my friends had lost their virginity years before, but I wanted the moment to be right. Finally, that moment had arrived.

My mother hated Mark. She said she just couldn't trust him. And she was right! After he got what he wanted, he dumped me. And if that wasn't bad enough, I found out he hadn't been faithful to me either.

Mum came home one day to find me in tears and with a bottle of pills. She held me in her arms and said that she knew I was feeling very weak, but she would be strong for me because that was what mums were for. My attempted suicide was never mentioned again.

Now I was a grown-up in my mind, I started to look for answers in my life. My parents had divorced when I was a baby and I hadn't seen my father since I was three. After much soul-searching, I decided to look for him. It was a long-drawn-out process, but eventually I found an address. Dad was the total opposite of what I thought the man who walked out on us would be like. He was gentle, kind and very pleased to see me and we began to catch up on lost years. Mum was obviously not happy about all this. She didn't say anything, but I could just tell. We'd argue about the smallest of things and we never talked about anything the way we used to. In fact, we were becoming like strangers.

My relationship with Mum got so bad that I decided to move in with Dad for a while. Mum's boyfriend Sean would call me and beg me to go back and patch things up, but no matter how hard I tried, it didn't work. One day, I decided that I would go and spend the whole weekend with Mum to give it one last go. As I drove to her house, I was mulling over in my mind what I was going to say to her, when suddenly a car sped out of nowhere and crashed right into me, it all happened so fast. Some passers-by quickly helped me out of my car, only to then watch as an articulated lorry crashed into my car again, and it burst into flames. As I watched in horror, I couldn't help but imagine what would have happened to me if I had still been inside.

The police tried to call my dad but there was no answer, so they called Mum. All she was told was I had been involved in an accident. When Mum arrived at the scene she saw my car being hosed down, and she automatically thought the worst. I saw her fall to her knees and cry, I saw the look of devastation in her eyes, and I also saw the look of love and sheer relief when she saw me walking towards her. We said nothing, she just held me.

After I was checked out at the hospital, Mum took me back to Dad's. I knew this would be hard for her as she hadn't seen him in twenty years. I'm not sure who was more nervous as I opened the front door. I switched on the hall light to reveal that the flat was empty, apart from my stuff. At first I thought we might have been the victim of some strange burglary. But then Mum found a post-it stuck on the fridge door. 'Diane, I am not ready to be a father, when I am, you will be the first to know.' Mum tried to comfort me, but I shrugged her off and gathered my things in silence. I couldn't cry, I was emotionally exhausted.

A few days later, I was coming out of the shower when all of a sudden it occurred to me what had actually happened. I had come close to death at a time when I was not at peace with my mother. What would have happened if I'd died in that crash? Not only that, but I realised that my dad had done the same thing to me as he did to Mum when I was three. He had run away just when we needed him most. That's when the tears finally came. It must have taken all Mum's strength for her not to try and influence my opinion of Dad. Now I knew why she had been so strange of late; she was just trying to do what she has done since the day I was born. Love and protect me.

Sophie and Tom

Sophie's Leading Role . . .

I first noticed Tom when I started secondary school, that's a long, long time ago now. Over the years, as we grew up, I noticed he was so unlike all the other boys. He was gentle and kind. His personality was in complete contrast to his friends, who seemed to be showing off all of the time.

And so I developed my first teenage crush on Tom. Like so many kids at that age, I became convinced that Tom was the one and only guy for me.

The school years rushed by and before you knew it, we'd sat all our exams and it was our end of term farewell 'prom'. Everyone was dressed up to the nines and trying to be as grown-up as possible. Tom looked so handsome in his suit and tie. When our eyes met I knew something was going to happen that night that I would never forget. Towards the end of the night, Tom asked me to go outside with him. My heart was nearly in my mouth at this point, this was the moment I'd been waiting for. It was pouring with rain outside, which made things even more romantic as we had to take shelter under a flight of stairs. I was so excited, what was he going to say? Or was he just going to grab me and kiss me? As we settled in our private hideaway, a drop of rain trickled down my forehead. Tom gently brushed it aside as he looked deep into my eyes.

'This is it,' I thought, 'he's going for the kiss!' Then suddenly he said, 'You're the first to know this, I want you to know my dream has come true.' I was waiting for him to tell me how he'd always had feelings for me, but instead he told me he had been accepted into a theatre school and he would be moving away very soon. 'I'm so excited, I wanted you to be the first to know.'

Well, they say that in your lifetime your heart will break a thousand times, well, I felt like I'd had my quota all in one night. Of course, I put on a brave face and hugged him and praised him on his 'wonderful' news, but when I got home that night I must have cried a river.

The next few weeks were a blur and I don't think I even said two sentences to Tom. On the last day he slipped a note into my hand and whispered, 'You're still my number one girl, always.' The note told me how much he felt for me but he wasn't going to leave me his new address because a long-distance relationship would tear us apart and he wouldn't be able to cope with speaking to me on the telephone.

I had to get on with my life and, as the years went by I met lots of men, but never really settled. One day, I got a phone call, the voice sounded strangely familiar. I couldn't believe it when it turned out to be Tom. He told me how he was sorry that he hadn't been in touch but could I go and see him at his house. 'There's that ego again,' I thought, 'If he wants to see me, why doesn't he come and see me? A couple of days later I arrived at a stunning house in Kensington. It was obvious his acting career had gone very well, even though I'd never seen him perform. There was a long pause before he arrived at the door. I was beginning to think that Tom was deliberately being dramatic, when he answered the door in a wheelchair! At first I thought he might be researching a new role, but later he explained that he had fallen off some scenery and was paralysed from the waist down.

Tom's personality hadn't changed a bit. He still had the best sense of humour. He still had the same sparkle in his eyes and he was still my Tom. I knew that I had never fallen out of love with him, and this time, I made sure I got the kiss that I had been waiting ten years for.

Tom's disability does restrict him slightly and he has his up and his down days, but as long as we are together I don't think it matters. Tom and I are now engaged and I am pregnant with our first child.

Lauren
and Jamie

A Case of
Accidental Love?

I was beginning to give up on men. I had never really been in a serious relationship. I suppose you could say a couple of them had potential, but I never fell in love with them. I wasn't the sort of person who would say 'I love you' to just anyone, so by the time I was twenty, I'd never said those three little words to anyone.

One day, my friend Kelsey said her friend from work was having a party and I should go along too. Well, of course, I didn't know anyone there so I ended up getting completely drunk. Through the alcoholic haze I noticed there was this guy who kept smiling at me. Well, at this stage I felt like I had nothing to lose so I went to talk to him. For the first time in ages I was talking to a man and felt completely relaxed. His name was Jamie and by the end of the party we had exchanged phone numbers.

Things moved quickly on from there and before we knew it we were living together. Fate seemed to be rushing us for some reason because not long after that I found out I was pregnant. When I told Jamie, he proposed! I was overwhelmed.

The pregnancy went well and when little Sophie was born my life was complete. Apart from those three little words. I had told Jamie I loved him, but deep down, I wasn't sure if I meant it. What is love? I thought, is this the real thing? I didn't want to end up getting hurt.

One night we were in bed having a wonderful romantic night and were talking frankly about our future. I was just beginning to relax when Jamie's job got in the way. He worked as a nurse and tonight he was on call. Our love-making was abruptly interrupted by the piercing sound of Jamie's pager. Reluctantly, Jamie got dressed and kissed me saying, 'See you, sweetheart,' and he was gone. He left me in a bed that felt especially empty that night. I must have eventually dropped off to sleep because the next thing I remember is being woken by the sound of a very loud banging on the front door. Uh, trust Jamie not to take his key, I thought.

I staggered to the door only to find a policeman standing on the other side of it. My heart skipped a beat, as I was shocked into conciousness. The policeman said Jamie had been hit by a drink-driver on the way to the hospital. I could tell from the look on his face that it didn't look good.

The rest of the night was just a blur. At the hospital, the doctors told me it was bad, but they were expecting Jamie to make it through the night. They were wrong. As he slipped away, I held his hand and whispered, 'I love you'. This time I knew I meant it, but now it was too late.

The emotional shock was immense. I was feeling so bad, my mother told me to go to the doctors. She ran a few tests and came up with the answer; and not one I was expecting. I was four months pregnant. Six months later I gave birth to a little boy, just like his daddy always wanted. He would've been so proud. I called him Jamie, of course.

I can't wait for Sophie and Jamie to grow up so I can tell them about their wonderful father and how I truly loved him. For now I keep a picture of him in my pocket, close to my heart, where he will stay for ever.

14

Ann and Gerry

It's All a Different Game in the Second Half

To say I wasn't a high priority in my husband's life was an understatement. David's first love was outside of our marriage and he made no secret of it. He lived for football. Over the years David must have broken my heart a thousand times and left me feeling totally inadequate. My only consolation was our beautiful daughter and it was she who gave me the strength to carry on with my life.

We had been together for thirteen years, but I could take it no more and filed for divorce. After the split came the dividing up of belongings and naturally, the house had to go. During the sale I met Gary. It felt a bit scary to be free to follow my urges towards him, but oh so great to be appreciated. I had a brief sexy fling with Gary. Neither of us wanted involvement and he particularly didn't want to get in too deep with someone with a child. After the sex died, we remained friends, but before long, lost touch.

A year after my divorce I had a major operation and was off work for eight weeks. While I was convalescing, my colleagues from London and our office in New York called me to cheer me up and keep me in the loop with developments at work. One day a new recruit called Gerry phoned from New York to tell me we would be working together when I got back. I thought how nice he sounded. Towards the end of my sick leave I went into my office to catch up with what had been going on. At that moment, my boss walked in with this handsome looking man and said, 'Welcome back Ann, why don't you join me and Gerry for lunch?' In the restaurant we all made polite businesslike conversation. Gerry told me he was a divorcee with two kids – I thought he was nice but did not think too much more.

Later that year I had to go to New York to work with Gerry for a week. I didn't think anything of it until one day when I had a problem understanding a project I was working on and I asked Gerry for some help. He leant across the desk provocatively and looked at me in a way that left me in no doubt about what he was thinking. It was a very sexy moment; not sleazy in the slightest. Suddenly I knew I had feelings for him, but I said nothing because we were far too busy.

That night we had to take some clients out for dinner. I was sure Gerry was flirting throughout the meal. After dinner, our clients went home and Gerry and I went on to a bar for a few drinks, which turned into more than just a few. The next morning, I woke up in my hotel bed with Gerry next to me. To say that work was awkward that day was an understatement, but again we were too busy to sit down and discuss what had happened the night before. Back in London Gerry and I continued to work comfortably together across the miles still never mentioning our 'connection'.

In August, there was a problem with my ex-husband. Gerry happened to phone on business that night, but remembering he was a divorcee too, I ended up asking his advice. This seemed like a good time to bring up the hotel incident. It really cleared the air between us.

In September Gerry told me he needed some advice from me. He said I owed him. Would you believe he wanted me to go over to advise him on how to decorate his apartment! Well, like he said, I did owe him, so I booked a flight. I flew over to New York in November. When we met at the airport, he just hugged me and so began the most wonderful year of my life. We were so lucky, despite living thousands of miles apart, we managed to arrange to see each other almost every month and speak on the phone every day because of our work. Our only worry was what if our bosses found out. We were sure they would frown on our relationship; after all, indirectly it was costing them a fortune. We finally came clean at the company Christmas party and to our surprise, everyone was overjoyed.

I have spent the best Christmas ever with Gerry, his family and my daughter. I'm not entirely sure what the future holds right now, but I do know I love him passionately. If he asked me to go and live in New York tomorrow I would have no hesitation. Wherever we live I know the future looks extremely bright.

15

Darren & Karen

Ninth Floor for Red-hot Passion . . . Going Up!

It was a hot summer Saturday night and I was out on the town with my regular crowd of friends. We went into a bar for a pre-club drink. It was a new trendy place that we had never been into before. Once inside, we started getting up to our usual antics, messing around and just generally having a good time. After a while, I looked around the bar to see what sort of women came into a cool place like this. There was no shortage of good looking 'talent', but then someone just stood out from the crowd. She was the most beautiful woman I had ever seen in my life. I nudged my friend Dave and asked for his opinion. He just laughed and said, 'Dream on Darren, there is no way on God's earth she would ever look at someone like you! Forget it!' Not long after that, my mystery woman got up and left and that was it . . . or so I thought.

The club we were going to was on the ninth floor and there was a big queue for the lift. My friends and I passed the time making fun of each other, not paying much attention to anyone else in the queue while we waited. Suddenly, I caught a familiar sight out of the corner of my eye. I looked around to see my dream woman getting into the lift. I pushed my way out of the queue and made a dash for it, much to the disapproval of the people in front of me. I squeezed into the lift just in time. As the doors closed, I could hear the cheers of encouragement from my friends as the lift started to ascend. So there we were packed like sardines in a tin. The advantage with a situation like this is that she could hardly avoid me. We didn't say much, we just stared at each other, she told me her name was Karen and that was it.

In the club and reunited with my friends, they had a saucier version of what must have happened in the lift. It's amazing what they imagined could happen during thirty seconds or so, but that's guys for you. A few of my friends went over to try to chat to Karen's friends, but immediately got the brushoff. After some considerable persuasion from my friends, I decided to go and talk to Karen. As I approached her table, I saw her moving to make space for me to sit next to her; I couldn't believe my luck. We talked and talked, in fact I became quite hoarse trying to be heard over the music. But as the night went on it became more and more obvious that there was an attraction there between us. I then gave Karen my phone number and she said she would call the next day.

It was four in the afternoon and by now I'd given up on Karen. I felt a little let down inside, I really felt like we had made a connection, but she obviously thought differently. Then suddenly my mobile phone went off with a text message. It said, 'Do you remember me from last night – do you still want to see me again?' I wondered why she had taken all the trouble to type this message in to her phone when she could have just spoken to me. Unless she was hiding something of course. I was about to find out. When I confirmed I was interested she sent another message saying 'Even if I tell you I am married with two kids?' I was really so shocked that this beautiful woman was married. I felt as if I had a right hard kick in the ribs, but I knew inside I had to see her again. We arranged to meet that Friday night.

It was a dream come true to meet someone who was so beautiful and just to click so well. That night, we went back to my flat and we made the best love in the world; it was just magical.

For the next few months we would see each other as often as we could and we were becoming seriously emotionally involved. By the time we went away for a weekend, I had fallen for her completely. I started to think that we could have a real chance together. We could set up home and have a child of our own. While she was asleep, I would look at her and think to myself, God, this woman is so beautiful – why would she want to look at me?

Christmas came and Karen told me that it would be impossible for her to get away as her kids were off school and her husband was also not working. So I went to my father's home for the holidays to try and forget about what she might get up to during the festive period. My dad has always had a perceptive streak in him and he sensed my anguish straight away. He took me to his local pub and began to quiz me. I'd been through this line of questioning as a child, so I knew there was no point in holding back. As I heard myself explaining my situation, I realised what a mess I was in. Dad hardly had to give me a word of advice – I knew what I had to do.

So after the holidays, I called it all off. I could not live with myself for wrecking a family. I know Karen's marriage had its problems, but I wasn't the answer, just a temporary diversion from it all. I will miss her so much and I will always love her no matter where I am or what I am doing.

16

Graham & Elaine

The Traveller's Guide to Romance

Nineteen seventy-four was my special summer. I think everyone likes to remember when they were young and discovering love for the first time. I was just eighteen and I set off to travel around Europe with my best friend Chris. Student travel wasn't as commonplace in those days, we felt like we were pioneers. Little did I know that I was about to make a discovery that would change my life.

Chris and I arrived in Copenhagen and it seemed like a very sociable place. That's where we met two female travellers from Canada. One of them was called

Elaine. She wasn't 'drop dead gorgeous', but something about her made me feel very comfortable. That evening we went for a walk and we talked and talked. I told her things about me that I had never told anyone before. I suppose I did it because I figured I'd never see her again, so what was there to lose? When I got back to my hotel room, I reflected on the evening and started getting a funny feeling but I didn't really know what it was.

We all made a happy foursome over the next few days and saw the sights of Copenhagen together. Elaine and I completely clicked. I felt so comfortable with her; it was as if I had known her for years. Then one night, we were having another one of our soul-baring conversations when she told me that she was engaged to someone back in Canada. She might as well have picked up a brick and hit me over the head with it. My only saving grace was my belief that I had the advantage because I was with her and he was thousands of miles away. I decided not to give up on Elaine and give it my 'best shot'.

After a few days we decided to travel to Stockholm by train. It was a night train, so I was hoping it was going to be a romantic experience. Elaine and I sat next to each other and we talked the night away. When the words finally ran out, I leant over and kissed her, not passionately, but I suppose you could call it an affectionate kiss. As I pulled away from her I said a little embarrassingly, 'I'm sorry, I didn't mean to do that,' but to my surprise she replied, 'Well, let me do the next one.' After that, only a few very intimate words passed between us as our bodies took up the conversation.

In Stockholm, I fell completely in love with Elaine. I knew somehow that this was a holiday romance and wouldn't come to anything, but she in no way tried to discourage our friendship and accepted my love for her totally. I wasn't about to stop my feelings for her. We spent a glorious few days together, but time was running out as her travel pass was due to expire and she really wanted to visit London before flying home. Through all our time together Elaine never told me she loved me, but I just knew the feelings were there and on the last day she proved it. She went to the shops and bought a really smart and expensive outfit and in her words, 'I want you to remember me like this.' We had a very sad final dinner that evening, where we hardly ate a thing, and then our last night together. As I kissed each part of her beautiful body, I wondered if this really was the last time my lips would touch her skin. In the morning, she left my hotel room without saying a word and checked out of my life.

Chris and I continued on our travels, but my heart wasn't in it. After a few days we made our way down south and stopped at Amsterdam. Strangely enough, we decided to visit the Alkmaar cheese market. I was beginning to wonder why the hell I was there, when suddenly from behind a pile of Edam, I spotted a sight that took my breath away. It was Elaine! It was such a joyous moment and I was so excited. Surely after this, we must have been fated for one another? After all, what were the chances of meeting again like this? I told Elaine how much I had fallen in love with her. She tried to put me off her by telling me the worst things about herself, but it didn't work. So after a while she gave up, she just threw her arms around me and we were reunited once more.

Elaine and I travelled together down through Brussels and eventually to Dunkirk. Our final farewell was to be at the docks. As her ship was pulling out, the scene was like an old-fashioned movie with everyone waving. Elaine was up on deck waving goodbye and then came the moment I will never forget. I was sure that I saw her lips form the words that I'd longed for her to say from the moment we met, 'I love you'. I stood there for what seemed like ages on the deserted quayside. Why didn't she say that to me when we were together? I felt in my pocket for the piece of paper she had given me earlier and held it like a precious diamond. At least I had her address and could write to her. 'This isn't the end,' I kept telling myself.

I decided to keep a diary of the rest of my journey. As I made my way down to Africa, I wrote some of the most intimate things I'd ever written and I sent it all to Elaine.

Not long after my return from travelling, a letter popped through my letterbox with a Canadian stamp on it. I scanned all six pages as quickly as I could, searching desperately for a line that would tell me she loved me as much as I did her. It wasn't long before I had tears in my eyes. She said she had written to her fiancé while we were in Stockholm and had told him about me. When she got back to Canada, he had asked her if she had been in love with me. He had picked it up from the tone of the letters that Elaine had been sending. He said, 'You were obviously happier with him than with me, so do you love him?' She didn't tell me how she answered that question. I wrote to Elaine to try and get to the bottom of it all. I even asked her to marry me, but I guess I expected too much. Now it was her fiancé who would have the advantage of proximity to Elaine that I once had. I kept writing to her and pleaded with her to write back, but she didn't. I cried every day for months and became a total recluse, I didn't want to go out or speak to any of my friends.

Two years later I could stand it no more. I went to Canada to find her. I knew the name of her road, but didn't have the number. But I remembered she'd told me she had a Datsun. Fortunately, it wasn't a very long street and there was only one Datsun. Elaine's mum came to the door. When I told her my name, she invited me in just like a friend she'd known for years.

How much of an effect had I had on her family? How much had she told them about me?

Elaine's mum told me she wasn't there, but her brother would take me to where she was working. Her brother and I got on so well it was unbelievable. On the way there he even told me that he knew where she kept all my letters. We got out of the car and my heart was racing. I had imagined this moment for so long. I expected her to greet me with a big hug and lots of tears, but all she said was a plain 'Hello'. I knew from that moment my dream was slipping away. Eventually we got a quiet moment together and she told me she had taken ages to get over me and if I had visited her earlier, something might have happened, but now there was no going back.

The next day I left her and I haven't seen or heard from her since. That was twenty-five years ago. Since then, I have never told anyone this story; not even my wife. There's hardly a week that goes by that I don't think about Elaine; the woman who changed me from an extrovert into a very shy person. I think I am happy in my marriage and I love my kids, but a part of me still belongs to Elaine.

I know for sure that one day we will meet again, and if our circumstances have changed, who knows, maybe, just maybe . . .

17

Jane and Adrian

When You Reach the Top, There's Only One Way to Go

I had spent five years in a miserable, exhausting relationship with Paul. It actually took me a whole year to summon up enough courage to end it. You would've thought that I would feel relieved after all that, but I actually felt lonely and scared to be on my own.

The day I had chosen to drop the bombshell just happened to be the same day as my best friend Nicole's birthday. She had booked a big night at this karaoke restaurant. The last thing I felt like was a night out with the girls. But I had taken refuge at my parents' house and when they heard about the situation, they produced a fifty-pound note and said, 'Go on, take this, get drunk, forget about Paul, have a good time.'

I ended up sitting next to a girl called Debbie. She spent the whole evening complimenting me and trying to get me to agree to a blind date with her boyfriend's best friend Adrian. I told her I wasn't ready to meet anyone new but she was having none of it. I eventually told her I would go on this date if she would just shut up about it (I was planning to duck out of it in the cold light of day). The next thing I knew Adrian just happened to stop by and I was roped into confirming this date for the following night.

When we met up, we actually hit it off. Adrian made me laugh so much; I didn't fancy him at all, but I thought he would make a good friend. Adrian was almost too keen to see me again and I think that put me off at first, but in the end we found our own pace and we started to fall in love. Three months later and Adrian asked me to move in with him. I knew this was a big step because I'd lived with Paul, but it was a first for Adrian. I was amazed how well we went together in that flat. I discovered he was everything I wanted in a man. He made me feel so alive and secure.

On our first year's anniversary Adrian took my

breath away by proposing marriage. I was so excited; I had to call all of my friends and family right away. My family threw us a massive engagement party out in the country set in acres of farmland. It was the most beautiful sunny day; I'll never forget it.

After a natural high, I suppose there has to be a bit of a low. Ours was that I got glandular fever and he lost his grandmother. Suddenly we were arguing more and getting really jealous of one another. I thought it was just a passing phase, but suddenly Adrian hit me with 'I'm confused about us and I want to call the wedding off'. I was totally distraught. Once again I took refuge at my parents' home. They tried to tell me it would be OK, but I had seen the determination in Adrian's eyes . . . it was over.

The next morning I was woken from a deep pill-induced sleep by the ringing of the telephone. It was a tearful Adrian, telling me he had made the biggest mistake and couldn't spend the rest of his life without me. So it was all back on again. Well, for six months it was anyway. Would you believe it all happened again! And four weeks later, another call saying he couldn't live without me. This time we had to get to the bottom of it and we decided to go to a counsellor to try to sort it out. On our fourth session Adrian came in and said not to bother about sorting us out, it was over anyway.

Well, that was all I could take; I hit rock bottom. I lost weight and I sank into a depression. I didn't even want to get out of bed in the morning. I contemplated my two disastrous relationships and mourned their passing. Suddenly I realised that there was someone out there who I'd been neglecting through all this – me! I told my friend I was ready to go out. I used the money I'd saved up for the wedding to buy my own flat and, gradually, I began to feel human again. For the first time in my life, I wasn't relying on anyone else and it felt good.

Since then, yes there have been men, some really interesting ones. I still haven't found Mr Right, but I have found a new love. I've learned how to love myself.

18

Joanne and Neil

When Friends and Lovers Collide

Neil was my best friend – we'd known each other for many years and were inseparable. We went everywhere together; pool competitions and even weekends away. But we were just friends.

I'll never forget that evening ten years ago when we were out at a club with our usual social crowd when suddenly the slow songs came on. Neil made a beeline for me, but there was nothing unusual in that because we always danced together. There we were having this slow dance when all of a sudden, Neil just pulled away and walked off. I couldn't understand it, he seemed fine up until then. I cast my mind back over the evening's events to see if I could remember anything I might have said to upset him, but I drew a blank.

A little later, I got talking to one of his friends who had seen what happened. He said, 'Neil will kill me if he finds out I told you this, but he doesn't want to be friends any more. He wants to be your lover.' I was a bit shocked to start with, but after a bit of thought I decided to confront Neil and give it a go. 'Who knows,' I thought, I could be friends with Mr Right.

Neil thought I was just teasing him when I asked him out on a date. It took me an hour to convince him that it wasn't some sort of joke. In fact, all through our first meal together he kept on asking, 'You are serious about this aren't you?' To start off with things felt very strange. Here I was having a relationship with one of my best male friends. When we touched I would think, 'Should we be doing this?' Not surprisingly, we were really happy together. We had such an advantage over other couples because we already knew we were compatible. Things moved on really fast and we rented our first home just four months later.

Neil worked a lot of long hours running a bar and I found it very difficult spending so much time on my own. But we got through it and saved hard for a big holiday in Barbados where we could be together all the time. We came back home to a bit of a shock on the doormat. It was a letter evicting us from our flat! We had been paying our rent but the landlord hadn't been paying his mortgage. This situation provided us with the motivation we needed to buy our own place. We bought a little two-bedroom cottage and we absolutely loved it.

Years passed. We had our ups and downs like any other couple, but we had a home to be proud of and a life that many people would envy. Both of us had good jobs and we had a lovely German shepherd called Jake; what more could you want? Unfortunately it wasn't enough for Neil. We both loved each other to pieces, but it just didn't seem enough to keep us together. I had only one idea as to what it could be. Neil had been brought up in children's homes and foster homes and I guessed he didn't know anything about normal family life and this was stopping him from settling down. I tried to do a bit of home therapy by getting Neil to talk about his family and I thought we made some progress when Neil decided he was going to have a go at trying to locate his family.

We managed to track down Neil's dad and even found out that he had a half-brother and a half-sister. It was the start of a new era in his life; one that I thought would bring stability to our relationship, but in fact it did the converse, it split us up. Neil and I agreed to go back to being close friends. This worked fine for a while but then he started a new relationship with a girl called Jackie. Understandably Jackie doesn't like me being around.

Just recently, Neil has told me that he is moving hundreds of miles away with Jackie and her family. I have a real dilemma because I didn't realise quite how much I still loved Neil. The thought of him being all those miles away from me with someone else is really hurting me. All I wanted to do was set Neil free from the ghosts of his past, but all I have succeeded in doing is driving him away.

Who knows what will happen in the future – I only hope that one day Neil comes to his senses and realises who truly loves him. Then maybe he can come back to our little cottage and appreciate our perfect little corner of the world we created together.

19

Julie and Charlie

Age Ain't Nothin' But a Number

I remember the first time I saw Charlie at the local disco. It was as if there was a big arrow over his head with a sign saying 'He's the one'. I should have followed my instincts and made a beeline for him, but I had to discuss him with my friends first. I was only sixteen at the time, so I never did anything without their approval. I know I should have been eighteen to be in the disco in the first place, but it was the seventies – the golden days of disco fever – and that's where anybody who was anybody had to be.

Eventually, I made what I thought was a subtle

move to get noticed by Charlie; I asked him what the time was and . . . it worked! I couldn't believe my luck when he called me the next day and before we knew it we were seeing each other every day. I could not believe I was dating such a cool guy. I let my emotions run riot and fell in love.

Charlie was a bit disappointed when I slipped up one day and he found out my real age. He was twenty-two and thought that a gap of four years was bad enough, but six was like a generation to him. Despite this, we carried on seeing each other and had such a wonderful time together. All my friends would tell me about the stupid rows they had with their boyfriends, but Charlie and I always seemed to get along so well.

It lasted a year. In the end the age thing just ate away at Charlie and he told me that I wasn't mature enough to have a proper relationship. I was dumped. I didn't eat for days; I was too sick with heartache, I thought I'd never get over him.

Life went on. I left school and was lucky enough to get a job in a shop and that's where I met Mike. He worked in the shop opposite, was exactly the same age as me and was the perfect antidote to Charlie. So much so that a couple of years later we were married, settled down and had a little daughter.

During the year I was going out with Charlie, I had become good friends with his mum and I still kept in contact with a Christmas and birthday card every year.

So when my marriage fell apart nineteen years later, I brought her up to date in my card. That year I woke up alone on my birthday and thought to myself how miserable the day was going to be. I picked up the small bundle of cards that had dropped on to my doormat. I noticed there was an extra envelope on the mat with my birthday cards. It was postmarked Bournemouth and the writing seemed vaguely familiar. It was from Charlie wishing me good luck for the future and went on to say he knew how I was feeling because he was divorced too. He wrote his phone number on the card in case I 'fancied a chat'. I was so excited I just picked up the phone and called him straight away. When Charlie picked up the phone, he recognised me too straight away and we chatted for hours. He reminded me of the old days when we used to go fishing together and proposed that we should go and visit our old special places.

We met at the train station. Charlie didn't look any different and despite the fact it was now twenty years later, it felt more like a week. Seeing him again after all this time felt so strange, but we just took off from where we left off. Now, of course, we were both grown-up and the age difference meant nothing. Best of all, the sexual chemistry that was working all those years ago was not only still there it was stronger than ever.

Our romance blossomed again and climaxed on millennium night. On the stroke of midnight Charlie kissed me passionately and deeply (I thought he was going to eat me!). Suddenly I felt something hard in my mouth. At first I thought someone's filling had come out. I spat the foreign object out rather unceremoniously and reluctantly looked down to see what had been in my mouth. What I saw took my breath away; it was a beautiful diamond engagement ring!

20

Mel and Jamie

To the Man Who Turned My Whole World Upside Down . . . Literally

So there I was at London's Paddington station. Not the sort of place you expect your life to change – unless you're a homeless teddy bear. I'm sorry to say I'm a smoker and I'm one of those thousands of employees who sneaks off to the smoking room any time I can get away with it. One day I was on my break when I saw this maintenance guy and thought, Ooooooooh he's quite cute. I tried to subtly attract his attention, but he didn't seem to notice me. I went back to the office ready to forget about Diet Coke man and got on with my work.

But then the next day, there he was again. This time some of my colleagues were in the smoking room too and they joined in on a group leer! It really was like being in one of those TV commercials.

Later, I tried finding out a bit more about this mystery hunk. It turned out he was working for an outside contractor and they were only there for a few weeks. The only place I could get any gossip on my fantasy man was from his colleagues who were also smokers. But you know what men are like, ask them a simple question and you get a simple answer. Basically, all I got is his name is Jamie and he doesn't smoke. The situation looked hopeless. Then one day Jamie made an appearance in the smoking room; he came in to borrow some money from one of the others. The moment he walked in, our eyes met and I swear there was a sound of Cupid's bow piercing my heart! During his brief appearance, our eyes kept meeting but nothing was said and he left after obtaining his loan. By now I was all fired up. I thought, 'I don't care if I don't know anything about him, I want him and I want him now!' Desperate times call for desperate measures: I scribbled down my phone number on a piece of torn-off fag packet and thrust it into his colleague's hand.

I really wasn't expecting anything to happen, but then not even two hours later Jamie called. He had the strangest sounding Australian accent. When I mentioned it, he was most offended because he is from New Zealand. Despite all that, we were talking for quite a while. I was getting quite frustrated, as he still hadn't suggested meeting up. Then his mobile phone cut off after his credit ran out. The following day, the contractors had disappeared and with them, Jamie. It seemed like we were destined never to meet.

Two weeks later, I had forgotten all about Jamie and was on a date with someone else when I received a really strange text message from someone at a number I didn't know. I sneaked to the women's loo to call the number back and find out who it was. I was so surprised to find out it was Jamie! He told me he hadn't called because he had moved out of town for some more contract work, but that he was coming to London for the weekend. This time we arranged to meet up and we had a really good night. Too good actually, because we got really drunk and ended up having sex. After that, I thought I would never hear from him again. (Jamie said he would call me the following night, but we've all heard that one before.) But Jamie called me the following afternoon to say that he really was going to call me that night. It was so sweet!

A few weeks later I was so into Jamie and wanted to spend all my time with him, so I left my job at Paddington and moved out into the countryside to be with him. Being a bit of a city girl, I thought that was the biggest move I would ever make, but little did I know about what was coming next.

One day, Jamie just came out with, 'Mel, I'm sorry I haven't told you this before, but my visa runs out in a few days and I've got to go back to New Zealand.' I was speechless. I tried to be grown-up about it and over the coming weeks, I thought I would get used to the idea. But the pain just got worse and worse. All the time I tried to act normally with Jamie because I didn't want to spoil our last days together.

I woke up in the middle of the night having had the strangest dream. I saw Jamie and I roaming hand in hand through a beautiful field. We were very happy and calm but the weird thing was that everything was upside down. In the dream I kept on trying to point this out but Jamie said it was just normal. Awake, I sat up in bed and contemplated the dream's meaning. Suddenly, I knew what I had to do. I got up and went through Jamie's things and found out his flight details. The next day, I was on the phone booking myself on to the same flight.

I didn't tell Jamie I was going with him in case he

tried to talk me out of it. I insisted on saying goodbye the night before, claiming that it would be too distressing for me to go to the airport. I can't describe Jamie's face when he saw me in the check-in queue, but it was a moment I will never forget.

So here I am on the other side of the world, in Auckland, New Zealand. Jamie really has turned my world upside down, but I have to say my decision to come here was the best I've ever made. Maybe that dream wasn't so weird after all.

21

Muchaneta and Josh

Muchaneta's 'Perfect' Match

One thing I really enjoy is a good girls' night in. About a year ago, all my friends came around to my flat. We had a bitch and a gossip, ordered in pizza and polished off a few bottles of wine. It was quite a night! It was getting late and by this time we were all pretty sozzled. My friend Chrissy noticed the computer in the corner of the room.

'Hey, have you got the Internet on that?' she asked. When I confirmed that I had, she said, 'Let's go on line and have a bit of a laugh.' We decided to browse through some of the lonely hearts pages and see what sort of 'talent' was on offer.

We were all howling with laughter at some of the descriptions of these men. But with the amount we had drunk, we would have found anything amusing. The next page on the screen was for a guy called Josh. As we scrolled down his list of likes and dislikes, a tingle crept down my spine. I couldn't believe how much we had in common. My friends noticed I'd stopped laughing and before long their attention turned to encouraging me to get in contact with him. Eventually I reluctantly sent him an e-mail just to shut them up.

The next day I was regretting it all, especially the cheap wine; I had one hell of a headache. It got even worse when I remembered the e-mail incident. I switched my computer on to read the worst of what this sad Josh guy had to say, but there was no reply to be seen. I was too embarrassed to tell my friends, so I avoided their phone calls all day. The next day I received a reply from Josh. I actually felt relieved, at least I now had something to tell the others. I looked at the attached files Josh had sent. I was thrilled to see that there were pictures. I paused for a moment before double-clicking my mouse to see what they were like. What if he's ugly, what if they're not really his photos? I thought. My computer teased me with its slow revelation of the images. First I saw hazel-brown eyes staring out of the screen at me followed by an athletic body that would have been better placed on a porn page. I drooled at the very sight of him. When my friends saw him they were so jealous.

I'm sure you won't be surprised to learn that after that, Josh and I exchanged e-mails every day. At first they were just brief notes, but quickly became flirtatious. It wasn't long before we had progressed to long outpourings of the soul in letters that were pages long. Eventually we concluded that we were 'a perfect match'. There was no getting away from it, it was time to meet up. But there was a slight problem. Josh lived in America. So we moved on to the next best thing, the phone.

I was sure that eventually I'd find something wrong with Josh because I am so picky when it comes to men. But everything turned out to be great. By now we were four months into our cyber-relationship. When I couldn't find anything wrong with him, I decided he was too perfect and he had to be lying about something. I decided Josh was a fraud and my imagination began to take over. I started to leave e-mails unanswered and didn't return his calls. When Josh did catch me on the phone he wouldn't stop talking about meeting up. My friends started to tell me to be careful because he could be 'some kind of psychopath'. I'm sure they were only joking, but I took it all very seriously and became too scared to continue. I told Josh I just wanted to be friends.

He took the bad news pretty well, but it wasn't long

before our communication diminished; now there was no passion, it just wasn't the same. Eventually Josh told me he liked me too much to just be friends and we ended it. It was only then that I realised how deep my feelings were for Josh. I thought back about the things we had said and looked at the photos he had sent of his whole family. I remembered how I'd chatted to his mum like I'd known her for years. How could all this be untrue? I realised what a fool I'd been.

A few weeks later, I just happened to be in New York on business. I had brought Josh's phone number with me, just in case I felt like calling him. This was my chance to put everything right and finally meet this dream man, but pride wouldn't let me call him.

I think I'm like a lot of people; I believe that there is a perfectly matched partner out there for everyone. Some people find their soulmate easily, some spend their whole lives looking and never find that person. I guess my fear is that I found mine and because of the modern world, I never had the nerve to meet him. My greatest fear is: what happens if he's the only one?

22

Rachel and Sam

He's the One!

I couldn't wait for the day that I was going to marry Darren. All the preparations for the wedding were going according to plan and I was in the middle of making one hundred and one arrangements for the big day. The last thing I expected was to find my future husband in bed with another woman. As you can imagine, I went nuts! I called him all the names under the sun and told him I wouldn't marry him now if he were the last man on earth.

The hurt went deeper than even I expected. I ended up quitting my job and I even sold my flat to get rid of the memories of this pig called Darren. Now I had no money and nowhere to live. I was left with no alternative but to move back home and live with my parents. This was a prospect I wasn't relishing, I had been on my own for so many years, I did not really want to go back to my mum's constant nagging and having to explain my every move.

Strangely enough, Mum and Dad gave me some space and they were really supportive. My self-esteem was, understandably, at an all-time low, but they were just the people to start my recovery. They suggested I look up some of my old teenage friends.

Sabrina was my best friend from schooldays and was particularly delighted to hear my voice on the phone, as we hadn't been in contact for so long. Sabrina insisted she couldn't possibly wait any longer to see me, and I should come round to dinner that very night. The only catch was that her brother-in-law would be coming, but she didn't really think he would mind.

I arrived a few minutes early in order to catch up with what had been happening with Sabrina and her husband Brian. We had a joyful reunion, where they showed off their kids, and I showed off my tan from my get-over-Darren holiday. It was great to see them again. Our reminiscing was interrupted by the doorbell. For some reason my breath caught in my throat. Brian went to let his brother in and I remained transfixed, staring at the doorway. I know it sounds a bit clichéd but as soon as Sam walked in and our eyes met, I knew that he was 'the one'. I had never had this feeling for anyone before, least of all Darren.

By the end of the evening Sam and I were chatting as though we had known each other for years. We left together that night, and never looked back.

Over the following months, Sam and I spent as much time as we could together, loving every minute. We never actually said the words, but I knew I was head-over-heels in love with Sam, and I hoped he felt the same. One day, as we were lying on the couch in his house, I told him about what happened with Darren, and promptly burst into tears. Sam was wonderful. He stroked my hair, and told me these things happened, in fact he himself was once engaged, but broke it off. Best of all, he told me it was not my fault.

Well, things just got better and better, until one day, for some reason I felt particularly low. When I spoke to Sam that day, I began to impose my insecurities on him. I told him I couldn't see any reason why he also wouldn't cheat on me. I hurled accusation after accusation at him, without pausing for breath. When I finally ran out of steam, Sam looked at me for a moment and then vanished from the house.

I haven't spoken to Sam since then. He refuses to answer my calls, or even read my letters. Looking back now I know I shouldn't have got so involved with Sam on the rebound from Darren. If only I'd waited.

23

Sarah and Gareth

Something so Wrong . . .

I guess you could say I was just another bored housewife. My children were away at university and my husband seemed to be more married to his job than to me. I had plenty of things to do, it's just that none of them seemed very important. Mike had promised that we would take a big holiday in the Caribbean as soon as his latest work project was over.

Having the holiday to look forward to lifted my spirits, but it also filled me with fear. Ever since I was a child, I have been scared of the water; I don't know what caused my phobia, but I decided I was going to get over it before the holiday. I had seen a poster at my local health club offering beginners' lessons, so I decided to take the plunge.

Gareth, the instructor, was much more mature and sensitive than I thought he would be. On my first lesson I had trouble just getting into the water, but was very patient and to my surprise I didn't run out of the pool screaming! Over the weeks, I diligently attended the lessons and discovered a new-found confidence in the water. Gareth and I were becoming really good friends without realising it. One day, we were just chatting on the poolside before my lesson when he announced, 'This week I'm going to give you the ultimate test.'

With that he picked me up and threw me in the water. I was completely disorientated; all I could hear was the swirling water. A wave of panic swept through my entire body and I started flinging my arms and legs hopelessly. Gareth jumped in and pulled me out as quickly as he could, he led me into the first-aid room and wrapped a towel around me. 'I am so sorry, Sarah,' he said, 'that wasn't very professional, I know, but I thought you could handle it.' I just threw my arms around him and sobbed with relief. When I looked up, Gareth was looking straight into my eyes. I felt another rush run right through me, but this wasn't panic. I should have been freezing; sitting there in my soaking wet swimming costume, but I felt very warm.

I pulled Gareth towards me, my move met no resistance from Gareth and we fell into a passionate embrace on the bench. What happened next was another lesson, this time in physical love. I had never reached the heights of excitement that I did on that day locked away in that first-aid room.

That night in bed, I reran the day's events over and over in my head. Me, married, mother of two teenage kids and . . . sex kitten! This wasn't me at all. Of course, this is where it all should have stopped. But I was hooked on Gareth and nothing was going to spoil it for me. We met in secret every week and during the coming months we explored every sexual avenue.

Before long, it was time for that holiday in the Caribbean. I'd promised myself that the affair with Gareth would be over by then. By now, I had real feelings for him and going away was the hardest thing to do. On holiday, after Mike had slept off his work stress, he began to notice me and, of course, wanted sex. It felt terrible going back to the boring bedroom routine I had developed with Mike over the years.

That night, over dinner in the restaurant, Mike said to me, 'There's something different about you, darling; you're much sexier these days. Are you having an affair?' I nearly choked on my fish. He'd found me out, what was I going to do? Suddenly Mike leaned back in his chair and just laughed, 'Imagine my wife having an affair; now that would be something wouldn't it? Ha ha ha!" I breathed a sigh of relief and just went bright red. As Mike got more and more drunk, he joked about it even more, 'Well whatever it is, I like it. You're much happier these days – yes, Sarah, whatever you are doing, keep on doing it.'

For the rest of the holiday I contemplated the future. Security with my husband and a boring life in the bedroom or divorce, disgrace and a great sex life with Gareth. Suddenly it dawned on me that Gareth had never asked for commitment. He knew I was married and knew my situation. Then Mike's words came into my head again, 'Whatever you're doing, Sarah, keep on doing it.' So I decided to take my husband at his word!

Believe it or not, my affair with Gareth has been going on for five years now and we are both very happy. Mike seems oblivious to it all, he still spends most of his time at work and I still service his needs on the odd occasion he notices me. So what am I to do about this situation? Well, I've thought about it for long enough and the answer is – nothing! Like they say, if it ain't broke, don't try and fix it!

24

Shellie and Matthew

shellie's First Love

I want to tell you about my first love.

It all started out in Ireland. I had a lot of family out there and spent a lot of my time visiting. On one particular visit, I hooked up with one of my friends for a bit of a fun night out. We had discovered that the local boarding school was having an open evening at their debating society. We thought it would be a great idea to go along and check out 'the talent'.

We'd only been there a few minutes when I got a tap on my shoulder. I swung round to come face to face with the most fantastic green eyes I'd ever seen.

The emerald beauties belonged to Matthew, one of the senior boarding lads. Apparently his parents were seriously wealthy international business tycoons, which is why he was in boarding school. Matthew and I got on really well and decided to become pen friends. After that we kept in touch by letter and phone for two whole years.

It was Christmas Eve and I was at home with my mum getting ready for the big day. Suddenly the doorbell rang. I opened the door to find Matthew standing there holding a beautifully wrapped present. Matthew wanted me to open it, even though it was a day early. It was a miniature porcelain doll. Matthew had remembered that I had collected them since I was five; it was a perfect gift, I felt so touched.

After Christmas, Matthew and I went out for a meal. I could barely eat anything, I just felt so complete inside; all I wanted was to be with him. It was the start of our true love affair. We met up whenever circumstances would allow it. Otherwise we sent love letters and spent hours on the phone.

Most people know that a relationship is really serious when they 'meet the parents'. I only ever got to meet Matthew's mum and dad once. When they found out I lived on a council estate and my parents were divorced, they obviously disapproved. They didn't say the words but I could just tell. Matthew and I didn't care at the time, we were in love and love conquers all doesn't it?

A few months later Matthew told me that his parents were making him move to Hong Kong with them because they thought we were too involved and it wasn't healthy for us at our age. We were both devastated, but were sensible enough to realise we couldn't carry on a long-distance relationship, so we went back to just being pen pals. Eight months later, I got a letter saying that Matthew's parents had forbidden him to write any more. I thought it was all over, but the moment Matthew got back from Hong Kong, he was on the phone desperate to meet up. As soon as I saw him I realised I wasn't over him at all and we had our first ever sex right there and then. It was perfect.

When Matthew's parents found out we were seeing each other again, they tried to put a stop to it. Now it was obvious that they didn't want Matthew to see me because of my background. The more they protested, the more we were determined to make it work. The whole situation put a lot of pressure on us and it made our relationship pretty volatile. One night, we had just finished making love when Matthew announced that he had to go back to Hong Kong with his parents; this time it was for good. His timing just made me feel so used and I got so angry, I threw him out of the house. My blood was boiling for ages after that and there was no way I was going to call him. It was up to Matthew to phone and apologise, like he always did.

But no phone call came, well, not from Matthew. One morning his mother phoned and asked to speak to me. What was going on? Had she finally decided that my poor background was good enough for her precious son, or was she calling to tell me to keep away? Her voice sounded less pompous than usual. It was soft, but broken, as if she had been crying. She told me that there had been an accident. Matthew had been run over by a speeding car, which was being chased by the police, and the unthinkable had happened: my Matthew, my first love, was gone.

25

Toni and Jill

Partners in Crime

Eight years ago, I was an experienced policewoman; I'd pretty much seen it all. By this time I knew that I was a lesbian, but kept it quiet. My family had raised me to believe this was abnormal and, as a policewoman, it was very much in my interests to keep it quiet; the lads would've had a field day.

One day, this striking looking blonde called Jill transferred to our station. It was hate at first sight! I didn't know why. Unfortunately for us we were partnered up together, which made our lives hell. Our first big case was a robbery. We violently disagreed over the details of the case and submitted completely different reports to our boss. When he read them, we were summoned to the office where we were given a dressing-down and told to sort our act out. We both said we couldn't work together and asked for new partners. He told us life wasn't that easy and whatever it was between us, we had to sort it out.

Over the next year, things went from bad to worse. We rowed all the time and earned ourselves quite a reputation around the station. One day we were both called to a robbery that had gone wrong. I was supposed to go into the building first, but Jill rushed in ahead of me and ended up getting pounced on. She got really hurt in the struggle and ended up in hospital. I felt so awful; that was supposed to be me. I rushed to the hospital to see how she was getting on, but Jill had left specific instructions with the nurses that she didn't want me to visit. I had to wait six weeks before she was back at work and I could apologise. Jill wouldn't listen and we carried on in our hate partnership.

Next we were sent on a two-week fitness course where we had to stay in a hotel. Jill made sure she was sharing a room with someone else. We spent the first week in serious competition in every task we were set. At the start of the second week, Jill's roommate decided to move in with her boyfriend, so guess who ended up in a room together? We sat in silence for about an hour before Jill launched into a big gay-bashing speech. She told me I was abnormal and should be ashamed of myself. I went to bed wondering how she'd found out my big secret.

During the night, there was a big thunderstorm and it took ages for me to get off to sleep. When I finally got off, I slept heavily. At about 4 a.m. I woke up with a start to find Jill in my bed! 'What the hell is going on?' I shouted. That's when it all came out. How she didn't hate me, she *loved* me from the moment she laid eyes on me.

It took three days for it all to sink in. I'd been so hurt by everything she'd done, I found it hard to believe she loved me. Finally, I kissed her out of pure curiosity. To my astonishment, it felt like nothing I'd ever felt before; like an explosion of passion. I wanted to bed her right there and then but held back for fear that it was all a joke and she was trying to hurt me again. I half expected one of the lads to come out of a cupboard, holding a video camera or something.

I held off for three months and then finally let go on a night when Jill wouldn't take no for an answer. Since then we haven't looked back. We haven't only found love together, but we've also learned not to be ashamed of our sexuality. I want everyone to know that I love Jill more than words can describe and I'm going to spend the rest of my days making up for lost time.

26

Tara and Tim

Tell Tara I Love Her

It all started when I was six years old back in California. I was playing on the family farm when I met a boy called Tim. We did the kind of stuff six-year-olds do, chasing and fighting and the like. And through that summer we became good friends, we used to sit under our special tree, far away from anyone and tell each other all of our hopes and dreams.

As we grew up, Tim and I supported each other through our first experiences of dating and gave each other advice. When we graduated, we had different dates to the prom. I really wanted to go with Tim, but it just hadn't worked out that way. After everybody went home I went to his house and we talked into the night. This was my big chance to tell him how I felt about him, but all I did was just sit there with him watching the stars and talking about our ambitions. I went home hurting so much because I wasn't able to reveal my feelings.

All through college I wanted to tell Tim how I longed to kiss him and feel his arms around me, but he always seemed to have someone with him. After graduation he got a job in New York. I was so happy for him on a professional level, but I was so sad to see him go. How could I tell Tim that I loved him now? So I just kept it to myself and watched him go on the plane.

Some months later, I got a letter with an invitation to a wedding; it was from Tim. Now I knew that I could never be with him and that we could only ever be friends. I went to the wedding. The bride looked absolutely stunning and I felt so happy for Tim, but when I saw him again, all my feelings of love came flooding back to me. I had to hold back, how could I spoil what should be the happiest day in his life? I tried to have fun that night but it was killing me inside watching him being so happy with someone else. On the day I left to return to California, Tim came running out of nowhere and said his goodbyes and how he was so very happy to see me.

As the years went on, we wrote to each other about what was going on and Tim would tell me how he missed sitting under our special tree and that they were the happiest days of his life.

On one occasion, Tim never wrote back to me at all. By the time I had written six letters and received no reply, I was beginning to get worried. Well, just when everything seemed hopeless and sad in my life, I got a note that said: 'Meet me under the tree where we used to talk about things.'

I was so happy to see Tim, but my joy was tempered by Tim's obvious sadness. In fact, he looked broken-hearted. We hugged until we couldn't breathe any more. Then he told me about his divorce. That's why he hadn't written for a long time. He cried until he couldn't cry any more. Finally, we went back to the house and talked and laughed about what I had been doing and caught up on old times. Once again, I was itching to say something, but how could I say, 'Don't worry about your wife, marry me instead!' Tim promised to come back and see me soon.

The next time Tim and I arranged to meet under the tree he didn't show up. I assumed that he must have been busy with work or something and tried not to get too upset about it. The days turned into months and I hadn't heard anything from Tim. I just assumed he was tied up with divorce proceedings and the like and didn't think anything of it. Then one day I got a call from a lawyer in New York. As he spoke, I froze to the spot. He told me that Tim had been driving to the airport on the day he was supposed to see me. Unfortunately he was in a car accident and he hadn't made it. I just cried my heart out. Why did this happen to a kind guy like Tim?

I gathered my things and went to New York for the reading of his will. When the will was read, there was one thing that was given to me: it was his diary. I didn't know what to think. Why was this given to me? I took it and flew back to California. As I flew on the plane I started reading. It started with the day we first met. He had written that he had fallen in love with me on that day but he was too afraid to tell me what he had felt. It told of the happiest time, seeing me and dancing with me at his wedding and he said he imagined it was our wedding. And how he had no choice but to divorce his wife because of his feelings for me.

The final entry said, 'Today I will tell Tara I love her.'

27

Tanya and Danyal

The Paris Mis-match

I suppose you could say that I had a fairytale view of love. I always imagined that the love of my life would come and sweep me off my feet and love me for ever. I decided I was going to save myself and stay a virgin until the day that I met my knight in shining armour.

Two years ago, I'd just graduated from law school and I went to Paris with my friends for six months to take a well-deserved break from London, and our families. The three of us rented an apartment right next to this brilliant nightclub and that's where we ended up on our first big night out. The moment I walked into the club, I saw an incredibly delicious guy standing at the bar. I remember thinking, I hope he's a regular because I'd love to get to know him over the next few months. As it was our big celebration night out, we got a bit drunk, but I think someone must have spiked my drinks because later I was completely paralytic. I couldn't find my friends and didn't know what I was doing or even where I was.

The next day I woke up in an unfamiliar room and a bed that I didn't recognise. I sat up with a bolt and then the full horror of what had happened hit me, because there in the bed next to me was the guy that I had seen at the bar. What had I done? I decided to make a run for it but, as I got to the door, I realised I was wearing his boxer shorts and a T-shirt. I gave him a firm shake to wake him up and demanded an explanation. Danyal (as his name turned out to be) said we'd had a lovely passionate night of sex together. I went mad and accused him of rape and all sorts. I just couldn't believe I'd lost my virginity in such an ugly way, and what's more, I didn't even remember it.

I calmed down after an hour and Danyal offered me a lift back to my apartment, after all I didn't know how to get back on a bus from his place – especially in a cocktail dress. Danyal asked if we could go to dinner that night so we could discuss what had happened the night before. He sounded so remorseful so I agreed, provided I could take my friends as well.

That night it was a bit awkward to start with, but as we talked I realised that we did have a lot in common. Later on we got down to the finer details. I told him I didn't believe in sex before marriage and that I hated him for what he had done. Danyal apologised but said he didn't regret it because he loved me from the moment he saw me.

It wasn't long before Danyal asked if we could start again and go out on a date. Half of me still hated him, but the other half really wanted him. I'm sure you can guess which side won!

Four months later and we were sitting in a restaurant when Danyal proposed to me. Just a month after that, we tied the knot. We're still madly in love and haven't looked back since. This year we're going back to Paris to buy an apartment – we love it so much.

So, the moral of the story is, be careful what you wish for, you might just get it! I got my 'knight in shining armour' – he just didn't sweep me off my feet in the way I imagined.

28

Hannah and Colin

Fancy a swap?

Nearly six years ago now I was married to Adam. Over the years, we had built up a friendship with Colin and Claire. We all got on pretty well, especially Claire and I because we were both pregnant at the same time. When the babies arrived we were a bit more tied to our homes, so we used to visit each other quite a lot – it kept us sane. As the kids got a bit older we'd do trips to the coast and have a really great time.

There was always a bit of flirting going on between Colin and me, which was all taken as a bit of fun, but I was beginning to have deeper feelings. Then came the day when we went to a party. None of us had to drive, so we all had a bit too much to drink. We ended up back at our house for a nightcap. Well, you know how alcohol breaks down your inhibitions. When the flirting started, we all got a bit hot under the collar. I don't know how it all started getting out of control, but before I knew it, Colin and I were in one bedroom and Adam and Claire were in the other.

Swapping partners seemed really funny and sexy at first. Colin and I giggled at the thought of what our relative other halves were up to next door, while we fooled around touching each other. We decided to go and have a peek to see what they were doing and that's when I got the shock of my life. There was my husband having full sex with my friend. I sobered up in a flash and burst into tears.

Not surprisingly, after that we had a bit of a cooling-off period; we were all so embarrassed. But after a while things started getting back to normal. I remember phoning Claire one day, only to find out she was not in, but I ended up having a long chat with Colin. We both admitted that both our marriages weren't going great and I realised that my feelings for Colin were as strong as ever.

All was well until the night I gave Colin a lift. There we were, just the two of us and inevitably we started joking about stopping off in Lovers Lane to get our own back on the other two. But then fate intervened when Colin accidentally told me to take a wrong turn and we ended up in a car park. We turned and looked into one another's eyes. I blurted out a warning to Colin to watch out because I had such strong feelings for him, but he just pulled me close and silenced me with his kiss. Not only did Colin make me feel like a teenager, I then proceeded to behave like one in the back of the car. I'd forgotten that sex could be that much fun.

We started seeing each other in secret on a regular basis. We tried to stop it on several occasions, fearing what we stood to lose if we were found out, but we just kept sliding back.

Colin and I thought our lives couldn't get any more complicated, but they did. Claire accidentally got pregnant! From the moment Colin told me, I didn't know where I stood, and I don't think he really knew just how much I felt for him. I was so confused that I decided to write it all down in a letter and gave it to Colin. When he read it, he burst into tears. He said he couldn't believe that someone could love him so much. We knew the sensible thing to do was to stop our affair, but we just couldn't.

As Claire's pregnancy progressed, she would phone me on a daily basis and tell me how happy she was. I didn't know what to say to her. Then I got some news of my own. I was pregnant too! I knew it couldn't be my husband's because he'd had a vasectomy and besides, we'd hardly touched each other in months. This was the sort of thing you read about in a story, it wasn't something that would actually happen to you.

I was prepared to give up everything to have Colin's baby, but Colin wasn't so sure. All he could do was offer to come with me to the abortion clinic and hold my hand. Without Colin's support, I couldn't go on. I thought about telling Adam it was his, but I couldn't face a lifetime of deceit. I cried from the moment I arrived at the hospital. And I was still crying by the time I left. Afterwards Colin admitted how guilty he felt, and how he dreaded the arrival of Claire's baby, because it would make him feel even worse.

The big day came in February, Claire was over the moon, and naturally wanted to share her joy with me. When I saw her perfect little girl, it just tore me up inside. Not surprisingly, it was all too much for me to take. I started to have anxiety attacks and had to be referred to a psychologist.

The only thing I had left was my affair with Colin, which continued (although I suspected that it was out of guilt and not love). More and more of our friends were beginning to find out about us, but by now I just didn't care who knew.

That summer, I had to go back to the same hospital when I had a bad attack of tonsillitis. Of course, this time, I was with my husband. Poor Adam couldn't work out why I was so upset about being there.

Fortunately I was sent home the same night, but Adam had to go to work and I was left alone. Colin came over to see me and for a moment my spirits were lifted, but he only stayed for a few minutes because he was about to go away for the weekend with Claire and the kids. I was so jealous and I felt so ill – this had to be the worst night of my life, and I was going to spend it alone.

The weekend was awful, each hour felt like an eternity. I sat by the phone in case Colin called. The phone finally went on Monday evening. I was so desperate to hear Colin's voice even though Adam was at home. I snatched the receiver off the hook. All I got to hear was a torrent of abuse from Claire – obviously the truth had finally come to light while they were away.

Claire's words didn't hurt that much. I had been resigned to the fact that she would find out one day, but I wasn't ready for Colin to tell me that it was all over between us. His words were so cold. There was no apology, he just said, 'We're finished.' The next thing I knew, Claire was telling everyone what had happened, but was leaving out the part where it all started, when she had slept with my husband!

So now I'm left with my life in tatters. It seems so unfair because really we're all as bad as one another. Somehow I seem to have become the scapegoat for everyone else's lack of judgement.

29

Mark and Lori

Mark Takes a Dangerous Gamble

Four years ago I found out my wife Mary was having an affair. I can't begin to tell you how I felt, especially as we had three children, whom I love to bits. The feeling of betrayal was hard enough, but that was just the beginning. First, I was told that I had to move out of the house and then to cap it all, Mary tried to stop me from seeing the children.

I couldn't believe what she had done to me. I had to start a long, drawn-out legal battle which went on for years. During that time the stresses became so great, I started to suffer from epilepsy. They got so bad, I was having a fit once a week. Eventually, I had to resign myself to not seeing my children until they were old enough to decide for themselves if they wanted to see their father.

After all that, you won't be surprised to hear that I gave women a wide berth. That was until I ran into Lori, who was the new receptionist at work. She really awakened something inside me and before long I couldn't stop thinking about her. I was sure that someone so attractive would have a boyfriend or a husband, but after making a few enquiries, I found out she was single.

Every day, on my way into the office, I would stop and chat to Lori. She was a bit suspicious of me at first; apparently I had a bit of a reputation! Eventually, I managed to convince her that I was only loud on the outside to cover up my shyness on the inside.

We went to an Indian restaurant for our first date and we really hit it off. Over the following months, a really great relationship developed. Obviously, as time went by, I had to tell Lori about my disastrous marriage and the problems I had with my fits. It's a good job I did because a few months later, I had a really bad one. Lori knew just what to do, she got me into a hospital as quick as she could.

While I was in hospital, I had another epileptic fit. This time the equipment was wired directly to my head and it located the area of my brain that was causing the problems. This enabled the doctors to offer me surgery. But there was a catch. There was a considerable risk that interfering with my brain could change my personality. Worse still, I could be left paralysed.

Lori really didn't want me to have the operation; she was so scared of the possible outcomes. We went away for a romantic weekend and tried to forget about it for a while. The moment was so perfect, I couldn't hold back, I asked Lori to marry me.

Back at home, the phone call Lori had been dreading came. The hospital was ready for my operation . . . if I wanted it. I held Lori tight and looked her straight in the eye, 'I've got to do it!' She hugged me back, but didn't say a word, she just cried and cried. I had to go, I couldn't go on living like this.

The operation lasted four hours. Afterwards, in the recovery room, I was encouraged to wake up. All I wanted to do was sleep. I could hear everyone around me asking if I knew where I was. They wanted to know if I recognised anything. Then one of the nurses pointed out Lori, 'Who's this?' she asked. There was a long pause, then apparently I opened my eyes and looked straight into Lori's. 'That's my love!' I replied. Lori beamed back at me. Finally, it was all over.

30

Angie and Pip

See You When You're Older

My story starts many years ago when I was only fifteen. My best friend Lynn told me about her cousin and how perfect he would be for me. I met Pip at Lynn's birthday party and he was more gorgeous than I could ever have imagined. We danced together all evening and, later, our lips met for the first time.

We were still very young, but even at that tender age, I knew there was something special between us. Our relationship blossomed, we saw each other every day for a year, but then Pip told me he wanted to spend more time with his friends. In an attempt to soften the blow, he said, 'Don't worry, I'll see you when you're older.' Looking back, I realise it was only normal for him to want to be with his friends but, at the time, it seemed like a big insult.

It didn't really seem like we had split up. Pip and I were still friends. I even went shopping with his mum and babysat for her on some weekends. Some nights I would stay over, I remember listening out for Pip coming home on his motorbike. More often than not, he'd knock on the door and come in for a bit of a chat. I was so cosy under my quilt, I used to wish he would get in with me, but he never did.

Eventually, I started going out with someone new. Things were going great with Graham until the day that Pip said, 'You know Angie, it's a shame you're going out with him, I was going to ask you back out.' I quickly dumped Graham and waited for something to happen, but nothing did.

Pip just carried on living his own life. When he felt like it, he would turn up at my house for 'coffee', which always ended up with us having sex. I didn't feel like I was being used, because I always felt like one day we'd be together.

Over many years, history repeated itself. Just as I would find someone new, Pip would turn up and spoil things. By the time I was twenty I had learned my lesson. I was engaged to a lovely man called Paul and I was convinced he was 'the one'. So when Pip arrived at my office on Christmas Eve, I was ready for him. He asked me out for a drink but I was strong enough to tell him 'no'. During the holidays, he kept on phoning and I found it really hard to resist, but I stuck to my guns. The next thing I heard was that he too had got engaged. I set a wedding date, then he set a date, it was as if he was just doing it all to tease me.

On my wedding day, my dad asked me if I was sure I was doing the right thing. I know every father is supposed to say this but in my case it had extra significance. I took one last look to see if Pip would turn up, but his motorbike was nowhere to be seen, so I pulled down my veil and said, 'I'm ready, Dad." Five months later, Pip got married too.

My marriage didn't last. By now I had moved out with my two young daughters. One day Lynn came round and told me she'd let my big secret out. She had confessed to Pip that I was still in love with him. Before I could strangle her, Lynn told me that Pip admitted he still felt the same way about me. It was as if a great weight had been lifted from my shoulders. But what was I to do? Pip was still married.

As luck would have it, I ran into Pip at work. I could tell by the look on his face that he knew that I knew about his feelings, but said nothing. We arranged to have a drink sometime. He smiled and said, 'I'll see you when you're older.' Pip was obviously holding something back, but what?

We never had that drink. I found out Pip's secret one day by accident. I overheard some of his friends chatting in the local pub. 'Have you heard the news?' one of them asked, 'Pip's in hospital with leukaemia – doesn't look good.' My chin hit the floor. Pip couldn't have cancer, he was invincible. I felt my body go numb all over.

I went nuts at Lynn for not telling me, but she said she just didn't have the heart to do it. I wrote loads of letters to Pip, but only received one reply. I couldn't go and visit for fear of what his wife would say; she always knew we had something special.

Pip died the day before his thirty-eighth birthday. I couldn't even go to the funeral. So my friend of twenty-three years had gone. I just wish I'd taken my chances and told him how I'd really felt back on that Christmas Eve.

After his funeral, after everyone had gone, I took a private moment at his graveside. I spoke for a while about how our lives might have been and then left flowers with a note saying, 'See you when you're older.'

31

Taylor and Andy

Who Dares . . . Loses

It was back in 1982 when I met Andy. He was gorgeously fit and so courageous, he came over as a truly inspiring character. I was immediately completely besotted with him and then he went and blew it all by telling me he was in the SAS. I thought, why does he need to lie? He's a nice enough guy anyway.

Our chance meeting had happened in a pub while I was on holiday up in Hereford. Little did I know this was the base town of the SAS and Andy was out having a few drinks with his regiment, mainly talking about their experiences in the Falkland Islands War.

But afterwards, when I had heard all this detail, I realised that Andy was telling the truth and he *was* in the SAS. I was gobsmacked, the motto 'Who Dares Wins' and the media image of these guys flashed through my mind. I took another look at Andy and tried to imagine him wearing a balaclava. It seemed impossible but I knew then that it had to be true.

Andy was a really lovely guy. We spent a few days together in Hereford but then I had to return home to London and I thought to myself, that's the last time I see him; I'm sure that SAS act works every time. When I got back I ached. I hadn't realised how much I liked him.

About a month passed and to my surprise, Andy phoned and told me he had some leave and could he come and take me out in London. We had a fantastic night in more ways than one – we spent the whole night making passionate love.

The passion continued and evolved quickly into deep love. Andy and I got married in 1983. I gave up my job and moved up to live near his base. The years flew by and we had two perfect daughters and times were great.

Then the Gulf War came along in 1991. Andy was sent out there just as little Lucy was diagnosed with cancer in her gums. Poor Andy was heartbroken and didn't want to leave her but duty called.

After he went we kept in touch by letter. He kept

on telling me how difficult it was to concentrate on his work while Lucy was ill. In one letter he said he was finding it so difficult that he just wished that God would take his life instead of Lucy's. That was the last letter I ever got from him. My Andy's body was flown home to be buried; I was devastated.

Not long after the funeral, I attended Lucy's next appointment at the hospital with her consultant. He looked puzzled as he looked through my daughter's blood-test results. Eventually he told me that he had never seen anything like it, but the results showed that there was now no trace of cancer in Lucy's body. It had quite simply disappeared.

It seems as if someone else must have read that letter.

32

Liam and Lynn

Love Lost – Love Found

Back in 1968 I joined the army straight from school. It was the start of a long military career.

It was only a few years before I met my wife to be and later on we had a daughter together, called Jenny. In the early days we were a very happy family, but with all the moving around and time away from home, we began to drift apart.

I left the forces in 1995, and tried to adjust to civilian life, but then the gap between my wife and me grew wider and wider. It was only a matter of months before we decided to split for good. Jenny was twelve years old at the time; she must've been devastated. But she gave me support and love as we sold the family home and went our separate ways. Jenny said she wanted to come and live with me. Fortunately, my ex didn't stand in her way.

After the divorce, I subsided into long bouts of depression as I contemplated my defunct marriage and redundant career. The more I thought about it, the more I began to realise it was my fault. Jenny was the only reason I had to live. Who knows what I would have done if she hadn't decided to live with me.

Jenny and I would go shopping every weekend. She'd get the food and essentials, meanwhile I would buy enough beer to block out the pain for the next week. I knew it wasn't doing me any good but it was my only escape from reality.

One day, I was working on the roof of my shed. While I was up there, my next-door neighbour called up to me and offered me a cup of tea. She too was working in the garden. As we made small talk, I thought to myself, what a pleasant woman. I'd never noticed how nice she was before because I'd never really taken the trouble to talk to her.

After that day, I found myself thinking about Lynn more and more. She was separated from her husband, so we had a lot in common. The more I spoke to her, the more attracted I became. I really wanted to ask her out on a date, but I assumed she just wanted to keep our relationship as friendly neighbours. I was behaving like a shy teenager.

The great thing was, my infatuation with Lynn was lifting my depression. One Sunday morning I was just parking my car after returning from the newsagent's, when I noticed Lynn washing her car. We made small talk as usual, but then I casually mentioned that I had thought of asking her out. She said, 'Well, all you had to do was ask.' That was it. That was all I had to say. Why didn't I do it earlier?

Since then, we have discovered an amazingly relaxed compatibility between us. In fact, I feel I already know I have found the *love of my life* right next door! Lynn has given me a new lease of life. I've stopped my drinking binges and I've started to laugh again.

Here's hoping that our children will get on as well as we do, so we can all live together as one big happy family, and put the problems of the past behind us to start afresh.

33

Marcelle and Ian

A Strange Arrangement

Ten years ago, I was a young spring chicken just out of school, when I discovered men. Dave was my first really serious boyfriend and I fell head over heels for him. I was still living with my mum at the time and she noticed that Dave and I were spending every day together. She suggested that Dave might as well move in, seeing as he practically lived in the house anyway. I laughed, but she was deadly serious. She said it was pointless paying two rents.

Dave took her up on the offer and everything was great. That was until Mum was told she had to move out of the house. We had no idea where we were all going to go, but Dave said he had a friend with a big place who might be able to help us out for a while. His name was Andrew. I remember thinking he must have a heart of gold because there was no way I would've been so quick to welcome in a bunch of strangers like us into my home. Mum immediately set about finding a new place for her to live; Dave and I had lots of early nights and my sister Sophie set about starting a love thing with our host!

Everything was working out fine until the day I met Andrew's best friend. Ian had fiery red hair and was so handsome he really turned my head. I found myself planning how I was going to end it with Dave, so I could try my luck with Ian, but a few days later I found out I was pregnant. The easiest thing to do was to forget about Ian and settle down.

So Dave and I got married and we moved out of Andrew's place into our own home to prepare for the baby. I thought I'd never see Ian again.

Little Josh was barely a few weeks old when Sophie dropped in to see how I was getting on. I expected her to bring Andrew with her but instead she arrived with Ian.

I tingled as we talked and I thought about what might've been if I hadn't got pregnant. One thing I didn't think was, why is Sophie spending so much time with Ian?

Life went on and over the years, I had more kids with Dave. Then one day, Sophie called with some news that shocked me to the core. 'It's all over with Andrew,' she announced, 'and when the divorce comes through, you'll never guess who I'm going to marry – Ian!' I was devastated.

By this time Dave and I lived in a big house and it was our turn to be hosts because Sophie and Ian needed somewhere to stay. Well, what could I say? Don't bring your boyfriend over here because I want him! So they came. I got to see Ian every day and my feelings grew stronger and stronger. I know it won't sound like it, but my marriage floundered totally independently of all this. Eventually, Dave left.

The next thing I knew was that Sophie was pregnant. Now I knew I would never stand a chance with Ian because I couldn't split up a family. Six months later, poor Sophie was rushed to hospital with complications. Tragically, her heart failed while they tried to save the baby and my poor sister died. But the doctors did manage to save her little daughter.

Now Ian and I were left in the weirdest of situations. We were living in the same house, bringing up my children and my sister's baby together, just like a couple I always wanted us to be. It was only a matter of time before the inevitable happened and my dream of being with Ian came true. It's not the way I pictured it all those years ago and if I had any influence over the situation, Sophie would still be here with her man and her daughter.

It's nearly two years since we lost Sophie, and Ian and I are planning to marry as soon as my divorce is final because we now have a baby of our own. My only wish is that Sophie is looking down on us and she is glad to see that Ian and I are happy together and that her daughter is being raised in a loving environment.

34

Karen and Bryan

He Only Popped out for Milk . . .

Being a single mother with three children, I didn't get out of the house much. When the kids were in bed, I'd listen to the radio or watch TV, but occasionally I would feel really lonely. One night I saw an advert for one of those telephone chat lines. I wasn't expecting to meet the love of my life on the phone. I just needed someone to talk to, just for fun.

On my first night, I couldn't help but laugh at some of the poor souls who came on the line, but it was nice to have some adult conversation for a while. After a few weeks, I became quite used to the way the chat line operated and therefore more confident. All of a sudden a man called Bryan came on the line. He was so different to all the others I had spoken to. He didn't have any prepared chat-up lines or corny jokes; he was just himself. Everything Bryan said seemed to be exactly what I was thinking, it was weird! We got on so well, we decided to take the plunge and exchange telephone numbers so we could talk to each other without spending a fortune.

Now we were free to chat for as long as we wanted. After that, every night we would talk for hours and hours about anything and everything. We talked about our families, love lost and found, and what we both wanted in the future. Most of all we had a good bitch about our ex-partners. Poor Bryan really seemed to have been dragged through the mud in his life. His divorce was so traumatic that he had started suffering from an eating disorder as a result. He told me that his wife didn't even want to see her son any more, it was all very sad.

Our nightly chats went on for a month or so. By this time I couldn't stop thinking about Bryan. I would spend the day imagining what he was doing and thinking of things to ask him that night. I realised that even though I had no idea what he looked like, I still really cared about him.

One night we were chatting on the phone as usual. It was about midnight when suddenly Bryan said, 'Oh,

I really must go out for some milk, otherwise I won't have any for tea in the morning.' I just happened to say, 'Yeah, I am all out of milk too,' and the conversation returned to more interesting subjects. But a few minutes later, Bryan wound up the conversation, which seemed a bit strange. Normally we'd talk until at least half-past one. I thought back to what I'd said earlier and wondered if I had said something to upset him?

I was just turning the lights out before going to bed when there was a knock at the door. I was suspicious as to who would be calling at one o'clock in the morning, so I put the chain on before opening the door. There was a hunk of a man standing there whom I didn't recognise. He just raised his arm slowly to reveal . . . a pint of milk!

So that's how we finally met, nothing like we planned but like some of the best things – spontaneously.

Brian was a bit quieter face to face than on the phone, but we soon got over our shyness. We started visiting each other's homes on a regular basis and before long we became inseparable and I fell deeply in love.

I had always said that I didn't want any more children after the dreadful experiences I'd had with my ex. But six months after meeting Bryan something strange had happened to me, I had a feeling inside of me that said, I want this man's baby! It was strange, not only because I already had three kids, but my youngest was about to start school and I was planning to get my career going again. When I told my family I wanted another baby they told me I must be mad and accused me of rushing into things. But I knew what I wanted, so Bryan and I started trying for a baby.

We had to deploy some rather acrobatic techniques to get pregnant, but we did it in the end. As soon as the pregnancy was confirmed Bryan asked me to marry him. We had a beautiful wedding in the summer. I gave birth just one month later. Little Bradley was 9lb 9oz and is so beautiful. Actually, we should have named him 'twinkle toes' because he was born with six toes on each foot! He's just had an operation to remove those extra 'pinkies'. I'm told everything will be fine.

Bryan and our five kids have now moved into a beautiful big house and we are all getting on so well. I feel immensely lucky, all I did was pick up the phone to relieve my loneliness one night and before I knew it, I had a perfect life.

35

Jimmy's Story

My Only Crime was to Love My Family

Way back in the seventies I met a girl who took my breath away. From the moment our eyes met I knew we would have a special bond for many years to come. Samantha was only three years old! It wasn't long before mum appeared and from the moment I heard Patricia's soft Irish lilt, I knew I'd found my love. By this time little Samantha was sitting in my lap and clinging on to me like she needed me. Patricia told me that she never saw her father and therefore she tended to be a bit clingy.

Within a year I had moved in with Patricia and

together with Samantha we made a very happy family. I had to work very long hours to make ends meet, but it was worth it because our leisure time was so rewarding.

I was on a rare day off and happened to be standing by the door when some serious-looking envelopes dropped through the letterbox. I took them to Patricia and asked what they were. At first she didn't answer, she just looked at them with a fearful look on her face. Eventually she told me she was on the verge of being evicted because she owed a fortune in fuel bills and rent. She confessed she hadn't said anything to me about it because she was afraid I would leave her. I thought for a moment about all the happiness Patricia had brought me. Then imagined poor little Samantha in a homeless shelter. Immediately, it was clear what I had to do. I dug deep into my savings and paid off all the bills.

I thought things would get back to normal but, later that same year, I came home to find Patricia in tears. She told me she was in trouble with the police because she had been caught forging a signature to take money out of an account that wasn't hers. This had all happened when she was desperate for cash before I paid the bills for her. She had just found out she was being prosecuted for fraud. Once again, I stood by her. I could understand why she had done it, I'm sure I would have done the same if I had faced being thrown out on the streets with a child. I hired Patricia a decent solicitor. I said to her that this time she should purge herself and tell the whole true story and then we could put this whole sorry episode behind us.

Patricia risked a big fine, losing custody of Samantha and even a prison sentence, but fortunately she got off with just the fine. Once again I bailed her out for the sake of our future together as a family.

Finally we were back on our feet and we could settle down to normal family life. Two years later we had our own little daughter Jennifer and I was so over the moon. Six years later I was working night shifts for a security company when I was attacked and seriously injured. I don't want to sound too dramatic, but I nearly died. Patricia nursed me back to health in a matter of months. But I never regained my physique because my injuries were so severe. Patricia told me this didn't matter and everything would be fine.

A couple of years later I got home from work to find Patricia halfway out the door with her suitcases. She told me she needed a break from everything for a while and left taking our two daughters with her. Later I found out that she'd been having an affair with a man at work. If that wasn't bad enough, he turned out to be married, so I was really concerned as to where they were going to live. I tried desperately to find them but had no luck. The worry was eating me up inside.

It was nearly a year later when I picked up the phone to hear Samantha's sweet voice telling me she missed me. As soon as she gave me the address, I was round there like a shot. It broke my heart to discover they had been living in a run down bed and breakfast. I told Patricia I didn't care what she had done and persuaded her to come back home for the sake of the children.

We decided we needed a fresh start. My brother lived in Spain and suggested we could buy a business out there and lent me a large sum of money to get us started. Patricia had always liked Spain, so she moved out there with the kids, while I carried on working in London until we had enough money for me to join her. I visited every couple of months and at first it was a big success. But when I wasn't there Patricia was starting to get into drinking parties with other bar owners and before you knew it, she was up to her old tricks again. I knew nothing of this until she started to neglect the business. By the time I found out it was too late and we went bust.

We had to sell our house to pay off all our debts and had to move back into my parents' house, as we had nowhere else to go. Mum and Dad gave us two rooms and never charged us rent. Patricia found a job as she hated the idea of spending all day at home. It was only a couple of months before she betrayed me again. I couldn't understand why she kept doing these things.

It was almost as if she was determined to destroy our lives. The moment we built something up, she would knock it down.

Patricia and I talked it through and we decided it was probably best if we took a break from each other. We remained friends during this time and after a few months our relationship really improved. By now I was sure that we would be able to get back together, so I planned a big holiday in Kenya for our reunion. But when we returned from holiday Patricia started to change again. This time she became abusive and tried to turn our daughters against me. Words can't describe how much that hurt after all we had been through.

Patricia left for the last time five years ago. Since then I have tried so hard to keep in contact with my daughters, but Patricia won't let me speak to them and intercepts my letters. Who knows what their opinion of me is now? They probably think I don't care, when the truth is, I care too much. I heard that Samantha got married a couple of years ago and since then she has had a baby. I am heartbroken not to have been part of her life during all of this. I hope that one day Samantha and Jennifer will be independent enough to form their own opinions about me and maybe I'll get to see them again. Until then all I have is memories and no one can take them away from me.

36

Melinda and Lisa

It's Never Like this in Central Park

I am so lucky because I have a wonderful social life. I am in a circle of friends that is a little bit like the TV show. We all love each other to bits and we really look out for one another. On the first Friday in every month, we all get together for dinner and gossip about anything and everything . . . well *almost* everything. I have known for a long time that I'm gay but I haven't yet had the strength to come out. This is the one secret I keep from the others although I am sure they've probably guessed by now. I've known them for years and I have never introduced a boyfriend to them.

So why haven't I come out? It's not because I lack confidence because I know that I can look quite attractive on a good day. My problem is that I am very shy and I don't really get to meet many other women. I had never had a proper relationship with a woman and didn't really know how to go about starting one.

At our next Friends' Friday, there was a new recruit. Lisa was training with my friend Peter to do his new job and he had brought her along. The rest of us giggled among ourselves because it was so obvious he fancied her. The problem for me was . . . so did I. I'm glad to say nothing really developed between Peter and Lisa, but I did want to keep seeing her, so I suggested to the others that she should be invited to join our circle of friends.

Over the next six months Lisa became a great friend to us all. We would go out on many nights, drinking too much cheap wine and talking about our hopes and dreams.

One night Lisa took me aside and asked me the question that none of the others had ever dared to. I had been dropping enough hints to her so this hardly came as a surprise. I had planned to ask her the same question but, when the chips were down, I just couldn't do it.

A few days later I had to take some time off work sick, in fact I wasn't very well at all. My friends all turned up at my flat to see how I was getting on and to cheer me up. They brought me flowers and hot chicken soup, which was very nice of them but I couldn't appreciate their company much because I felt like death. Before long everyone made their excuses and left except Lisa. She seemed really sympathetic and stopped behind to chat some more and spoon-feed me my dinner. It got so late we fell asleep on the lounge floor together. Lisa cuddled me all through my restless feverish night and made me feel so much better.

When I woke up, Lisa had already gone to work. My mind did likewise: was that a cuddle from a friend or was it a cuddle from a lover? I wondered. I spent the whole day trying to work out what to do next. I was too shy to just phone her up and ask her and even if I could, I didn't want to risk scaring off the best friend I had ever had. I thought about the various rumours that had circulated about Lisa's love life and they were all about things she had allegedly done with men. The more I thought about it, the more confused I became.

Friends' Friday in February was coming up. We all decided to exchange Valentine's cards on the night, so I took the opportunity to try and find out more about Lisa's feelings without being too obvious. I wrote, 'Lisa, I really care for you deeply and I'm glad you're part of my life'; I also sprayed the card with her favourite perfume for good measure. I was watching her like a hawk from the moment she picked up the envelope. I could see she recognised the perfume immediately and after reading my message, she looked straight over at me and smiled sweetly. Throughout dinner we glanced across the table at one another and I could feel a real atmosphere building between us. When it came to saying goodbye, everyone was kissing. Lisa and I were the last to embrace, I was about to peck her cheek when she gently placed her palms on either side of my face and with that planted her lips on top of mine for a full-on kiss!

Surely now there could be no more uncertainty, but unfortunately Lisa was going away on business the following day, so we didn't get to speak. When she got back she was really busy and missed the next few Friends' Dinners. During that time, my insecurities have been playing on my mind and I have now come to the conclusion that maybe she wasn't as serious after all and our flirting was just a bit of fun for her. I hope one day I find out the truth but, for now, my love life with Lisa will have to remain a fantasy.

37

Ayeshia's Story

I Found My Ray in the sunshine

I was proud of my relationship with Richard because we really trusted each other. When we were together we were very close, but we also had our own friends and occasionally we liked to socialise with them on our own. Richard wanted to go on holiday with his friends, which was fine by me because I wanted to go skiing without him in the winter. I didn't worry about what he was up to while he was away, I was too busy thinking about what I was going to do to him when I got him back in bed with me! But our 'welcome home' sex was a bit of a let-down because something was missing. I still didn't suspect anything until Richard carelessly (or deliberately) left his holiday photographs lying around the flat. There were various girls I didn't recognise in the pictures, but a woman's intuition told me that one in particular had been sleeping with Richard. When I confronted him with the evidence, he didn't deny it.

It was very difficult to walk away. Richard and I had such plans together, we shared a lovely home and I had never considered life without him. But his betrayal of my trust had ruined everything and I knew I would never be able to forgive him. The only way I could make the break was not just to leave him, but also my job and England.

I applied for a job as a holiday rep in Greece and got accepted. It took a while, but when I eventually settled into my new surroundings and made new friends, I felt on top of the world. The best part was that I had found me again; I liked to work hard, play hard and make friends with loads of new people.

I shared my apartment with two girls, Tricia and Mandy. Tricia made it clear to everyone that we were not interested in men because we were both nursing broken hearts; all we wanted was to be footloose and fancy free. Another rep called Ray became our good friend. He was reliable and trustworthy and most of all, a good listener. He would let me rattle on for hours about how badly I had been treated by Richard, in fact he was the only one who would listen. My friends adored Ray too, even my mum and dad said they liked him when they came over for a holiday.

Towards the end of the season, Ray told me how much he liked my flatmate Mandy. I was pleased for them both and didn't feel a bit jealous when they started dating but then Mandy told me that she didn't really feel anything for Ray, she was just using him for sex. I knew how much it would hurt Ray if he found out, but I felt worse not being able to tell Ray before he got in too deep. The more I saw of them together, the more upset I got, but I couldn't work out why I was that concerned; they were two consenting adults and it was none of my business what they got up to. I suppose it boiled down to that trust thing again. Neither of them was being unfaithful, but I felt like Ray had trusted his heart to Mandy and she wasn't looking after it. I could do a much better job, I concluded . . . That was it! That's why I felt so bad about the situation; I was infatuated with Ray and I hadn't realised it until now.

Autumn was here and the holiday season was over and so was Mandy and Ray's fling. Back in London, we all kept in contact, but Ray and I still saw each other every day because we lived nearby. Ray would often come and stay with me at my parents' house for weekends and we would have such fun together. Now the coast was clear, I wanted to tell him how I felt but I was scared he would reject me and I would lose my best friend too.

One Saturday evening we went out to a reunion party for everyone from Greece. What a night! Afterwards, Ray was going to stay over at my place. We kept a friendly eye on each other all evening, just as we always did. Secret smiles passed between us all night. Towards the end of the night, as I downed a few more drinks than I usually would I began to gain a lot more courage. I decided tonight was going to be the moment of truth. Ray went into the hall to say goodnight to people and when he returned, I grabbed him! 'It's now or never,' I slurred and kissed him. He did not reject me, despite the alcohol on my breath. In fact he held me so tightly I could hardly breathe. The room spun around, our kiss continued for what seemed like hours, but I didn't want it to end, Ray's lips were softer than I had ever imagined. I was so glad he was staying at my place that night.

In the morning, I felt like a big weight had been lifted from my shoulders, despite having the hangover from hell. Ray told me how he had always wanted to tell about his feelings for me, but was scared of the strong person I'd become after getting over Richard.

Ray and I have now been a couple for a year and I have never felt so in love. I now know why people use the term 'the other half'. He is the half that I have been missing all my life. Now I am complete.

38

Bethany and Rob

It Was Only a Hug, But It Changed My Life

Twelve years ago I was at that very delicate age when I was just beginning to take an interest in boys. So when my parents announced that we were moving to a small village out in the countryside, my heart sank.

I had to start at a new school and make new friends. Fortunately, I met Rob. He wasn't like a normal teenager; he helped me out by introducing me to everyone he knew and making sure I was accepted into the crowd. I could tell Rob was different because my parents really liked him too and before you knew it, I had a full-blown crush on him.

The problem with being a teenager is that you are so inexperienced and sensitive about relationships, it's difficult to make any decisions. I suppose that's why most kids that age ask their friends' advice. I didn't feel like I could talk to anyone about Rob, just in case I was treading on someone's toes. I couldn't pluck up the courage to say anything to Rob about the way I felt for fear that I might ruin a wonderful friendship. One day I was trying to tell Rob I wanted to go out on a date with him without actually saying the words. I was feeling more embarrassed and tongue-tied by the second. Suddenly Rob moved closer and hugged me affectionately. With that he said, 'We'll always be friends, Bethany.' He'd got the message all right and the answer was obviously, 'No thank you, Bethany, I don't want to be your boyfriend, but we can stay as friends.'

So friends it was. Rob and I would go to the movies, visit each other's homes and go for walks together just like boyfriend and girlfriend. No one ever believed it was a platonic relationship, but it was.

By the time I was taking my A Levels, life had become very hard. My mum had developed cancer and eventually we lost her. Rob was there for me every step of the way through my grieving, providing a hug and a cheery smile whenever I needed one.

Neither Rob nor I had dated anyone else since the day we met. I hadn't even considered it. I wondered how I would feel if Rob did start seeing someone because by now I was in no doubt that I really loved him. My friends told me I should make my move and get on with it because we were obviously made for each other, but I kept on thinking about that hug all those years back and how he said we'd be friends. My sister had her own advice: 'You two should get drunk and just do it, you'll feel much better afterwards!'

Nothing had happened by the time we both went to university . . . different universities. In fact we were one hundred and fifty miles apart. Inevitably we lost touch during those years and had lots of new experiences with new people. While I was away, my dad moved house to another village. When I graduated, I moved back in with him and set about planning my future. During the autumn there was a lot of really heavy rain. I was stuck indoors and felt so claustrophobic. I was cooped up in a house that wasn't my home and I felt like I had to get out otherwise I would go mad. I decided to go for a drive; I didn't care where. Something pointed the car in the direction of our old home. I pulled up at the foot of the drive and peered through the rain at the house that held so many memories for me. My eyes diverted to Rob's place just across the road. It looked so warm and inviting, I felt compelled to go inside. I wondered if Rob's parents still lived there. Well, there was only one way to find out.

I was greeted with a warm hug from Rob's mum who said, 'I'm so glad you came, Rob's here, he's recovering from meningitis.' She pointed upstairs, 'He's in bed, why don't you go up and see him?' Entering his bedroom I was confronted by a gallery of photographs of the two of us together. As I looked around the walls, I could see a pictorial documentary of our lives. Rob was asleep on his bed, so I didn't disturb him. On his bedside table I noticed a letter addressed to me. I scanned the pages and it seemed to be mainly news and stuff, but then my eyes darted to the end of the letter, 'Bethany, I really miss you, I LOVE YOU!' Suddenly, I heard Rob's gentle voice behind me whispering, 'Bethany, is that you?'

For the first time in twelve years . . . we kissed! Three days later we were engaged!

39

Emily and Mark

I Believe in Fairytales . . . Don't You?

Back when I was a schoolkid, I was a firm believer in romance and fairytale relationships. I was still too young to have been in love, but I believed that when I found my soulmate, it would be like one of those old-fashioned romantic movies. You know, his eyes would meet mine and we would both know in our hearts that we were destined to be together for ever.

I was only in the third form when I went to see my friends taking part in the school music concert. It was a pretty boring evening really. The orchestra played out of tune, as usual, and our music teacher went bright red every time someone hit a bum note. Towards the end of the evening, the school choir performed. I have to say I was beginning to drop off at this point until I spotted this gorgeous looking guy in the front row of the choir. My insides did a somersault as I imagined what he would be like to talk to.

Over the next few days, I did my best to find out who this Adonis was. It turned out his name was Mark and he was in the upper-sixth form, which meant he was four years older than me. Remember, when you're at school, four years is an age gap that seems like a generation. I also found out that Mark already had a girlfriend in the same year and everyone said she was gorgeous. I might have been young at the time, but I wasn't stupid; I knew there was no way I was ever going to get to talk to Mark, let alone go out with him.

But fate was about to play more tricks on me because both Mark and I had signed up to go on the school music trip to Austria and his girlfriend hadn't. The journey gave us plenty of time to get to know one another and during our week away we had a fantastic time messing about. He thought it was funny that I was so much younger than him and he used to call me 'little girl', so I would retaliate with 'old man.' By the time we returned, I was in love with Mark but of course, he didn't know. Mark hadn't made any advances towards me during the holiday but I had fantasised that he had and it felt great.

Now it was back to school and back to the real world. Mark was back with his girlfriend. A few weeks later, we had a music trip reunion party at a friend's house. Mark and I danced together for what seemed like ages but then the slow songs came on. Mark gently danced me into the hallway and, before you knew it, we were alone, staring into one another's eyes. I was just moments away from my first kiss.

The following day I was on cloud nine. In the playground, none of my friends would believe I'd 'snogged a sixth-former' but I knew it was true and I was indeed on cloud nine! My euphoria wasn't to last. When I saw Mark he told me that the kiss was all a big mistake and he was sorry, but it wouldn't happen again because he had a girlfriend already. Soon after that he left school and I grew out of my crush.

By the time I entered my twenties, I'd had my fair share of love and heartbreak, but somewhere in the back of my mind, I still believed true love would be like a fairytale. During the summer I bumped into an old college friend who invited me up to Lancashire for a couple of weeks' holiday. She was house sitting this beautiful cottage for her cousin who was abroad on business. When we got there I was sorting out the mess in the spare room so I could have somewhere to sleep when I tripped over an old violin case, which seemed strangely familiar and, for the first time in years, thoughts of Mark entered my mind. I told myself not to be so stupid – the fact that there was a violin case in the room didn't mean that this wonderful cottage belonged to Mark: it would be too much of a coincidence. I put the thought out of my mind and set about enjoying a wonderful week in the sun.

But little did I know, fate was about to intervene in my life for a third time. My friend had overdone it on the sunbathing and had managed to get sunstroke, so we had to stay for a couple more days while she recovered. That evening I was in the kitchen preparing the dinner when I was overwhelmed by a sense of *déjà vu*. I looked up at the doorway to see Mark standing there. It took a moment, then the penny dropped and with it, his suitcase. He rushed over to me and hugged and whispered, 'It's been a long time, little girl.' This was the fairytale moment I'd dreamed all my life. I'd found my love.

40

Alison and Adam

I Was Living Right Next Door to an Angel

I was only seven when Adam's family moved in next door. He was three years older than me, which is a lot when you are a kid. My parents struck up a good friendship with their new neighbours, so Adam and I were encouraged to play together and before long we could be found in one another's houses practically every day.

The years passed and we seemed to grow up so quickly; we gradually discarded our toys and began to take more of an interest in one another's personalities. Adam discovered girls long before I was into boys, but he would always tell me about his experiences. I remember thinking it was really funny when he told me about his first kiss with a girl. Despite the fact that I had no experience with boys, I tried to be grown-up and give Adam my best advice about what girls wanted. Adam helped me along with my first boyfriend too and during that time we forged a special bond that couldn't be broken. The more we became involved in our love lives, the less time we spent with each other and a couple of years later we lost touch altogether because Adam moved into his own flat.

During my teens, I went through a particularly rebellious stage and as a result, I fell in with a bad lot. I thought it was cool to be friends with people that others were scared of. I dressed like a slut and swore like a trooper; in fact I earned myself quite a reputation. Eventually I became intolerable to my family, but nothing they could say or do would bring me out of it. My parents were so desperate, they asked Adam to come and talk to me. When he heard what I was doing, he was furious and came over to give me a piece of his mind. I don't know why, maybe it's because Adam wasn't an authority figure in my life but, for the first time in ages, I actually listened to what was being said to me. I cleaned up my act, changed my image and dumped my so-called friends. I had to admit, I was so much happier as a result and ultimately relieved because my former friends ended up in prison.

My first really serious boyfriend was Nick. He was a New Zealander and seemed to be besotted with me. We got serious very quickly and to be honest, I felt a bit stifled by it all. So when Nick told me that he had to fly home to spend time with his dying father, I was sympathetic, but secretly relieved. Nick begged me to go to New Zealand with him, but I pointed out that it was a private time and he should spend as much quality time with his father as possible, without feeling the need to look after me as well. Besides it was impossible for me to get the time off work.

I couldn't help but breathe a little selfish sigh of relief after I'd seen Nick off at the airport. Finding myself at a loose end, I got back in touch with Adam. He had just split up with his latest girlfriend, so he had time on his hands too. We started hanging out together an awful lot, just because we had nothing else better to do. One night, I was so bored, I descended on Adam's flat with a game of Monopoly and a bottle of wine. Upon catching sight of the box he groaned, 'I hope you're not going to cry if you lose, like you used to!' To start with, it was just like being kids all over again, but getting back in touch with all those childhood feelings reminded me of how close we once had been. As the wine eroded my inhibitions, I began to feel a yearning to hold my darling Adam. The crunch came when Adam landed on Park Lane and had to hand over all his cash. As he did I thanked him with a kiss, which in turn ignited a big fire of passion that had been building up for years. Before we knew it, we were on the couch and nothing was going to stop us going all the way. I couldn't wait to feel our naked skin touching and my senses were peaking in anticipation. Suddenly, the atmosphere was interrupted by the sound of a key in the lock as Adam's flatmate came in. Instinctively, we jumped apart like two naughty schoolkids.

In the cold light of day, I felt embarrassed but couldn't stop thinking about what had happened. Adam and I avoided each other like the plague. I don't know why, I guess it was because we'd crossed the line between friendship and lovers and never quite tied up the loose ends. The next thing I knew Nick was back from New Zealand asking me to marry him. I felt so sorry for him and a little guilty. He had lost his father and now he needed some emotional support from me. All I could think of was how I'd betrayed him while he was away. So, for all the wrong reasons, I agreed to marry him.

Nick wanted a short engagement so, before I could blink, all the arrangements for the wedding were well under way. When Adam received his invitation he congratulated me, but seemed a little distant. I knew there was unfinished business between us, but what could I say now? There was no going back.

It was the night before the wedding, I was back at my

parents' house trying to have an early night but not having much luck getting off to sleep. I heard the doorbell go and soon after some voices. I assumed it was one of the neighbours calling to wish me well. But then I heard someone coming up the stairs and Adam's face appeared around my bedroom door. He'd obviously been crying, so I beckoned him over to sit on the bed. He kept on going on about not wanting to ruin our big day, but I insisted he told me what was upsetting him so much. He told me I wasn't going to like it, but my mind was made up. Adam slowly started to reveal the contents of his heart; how he'd always had a soft spot for me ever since we were kids and he, like me, had felt there was a special bond. But it was only when 'the Monopoly incident' occurred that everything fell into place. He begged me not to go through with the wedding because he loved me. Adam pulled me towards him and kissed me, oh so gently. All the unfinished feelings of passion from that night on the couch came flooding back, but this time they weren't fuelled by alcohol. There was a long silence while we just sat there and hugged. Eventually I had to say something, I told Adam that it didn't matter what either of us thought, it was too late for me to back out of the wedding, too many people were coming and too much money was involved for me to just call it all off. And there were Nick's feelings to think of too. Adam didn't put up much of a fight after that, he apologised for intruding and left quietly.

My mind was buzzing all night. I contemplated my happy childhood with Adam and considered the consequences of calling off the wedding. I also analysed my relationship with Nick and the truth became clear. I staggered down the stairs at six o'clock in the morning only to meet my mother and father in the kitchen; they knew something was up and now I had to tell them. The wedding was off. Mum and Dad took it surprisingly well, but I supposed they must have put two and two together when Adam had visited the night before. Dad told me to forget about the money, all he wanted was for me to be happy.

I had cleared one emotional hurdle, but the biggest was yet to come. Poor Nick took the news so badly. I tried to let him down gently by telling him I wasn't ready for such a big commitment, but he was having none of it; I had to tell him the truth. Nick's face turned red with anger as I told him about Adam and instead of crying as I expected, he lashed out and hit me in the face. He bellowed obscenities at me and told me to get out or he would kill me. I ran as fast as I could.

I rushed into the arms of the boy next door whom I had loved for most of my life without realising it.

It's now coming up to our second anniversary, and we have a beautiful three-month-old daughter. I hope that Adam knows just how much I love him, and how grateful I am that he rescued me by loving me so much.

41

Chloe and Wayne
Patience Is a Virtue

I was just fifteen years old when I met Wayne. While everyone else at school was changing partners every few weeks or months, for some reason Wayne and I were more mature and our relationship kept going. We had been dating for four years when Wayne asked me to marry him. I didn't know what to say because I hadn't even thought about settling down so soon. All I wanted to do was have fun, go to parties and 'find myself'. Sadly, I had to turn Wayne down. After that, I couldn't blame him for dumping me.

Life was much harder on my own than I thought. I

missed having a man to hold and didn't have much luck finding someone new. My best friend Maria, meanwhile, was the first to get married. Unfortunately, it wasn't long before Luke and she were on the rocks. At this point, most 'best friends' would provide a shoulder to cry on, but not me; I started sleeping with Luke!

My sordid affair with Luke went on in secret for two whole years. The only person who knew about it was Wayne and he kept on telling me to end it before Maria found out, but I didn't listen and eventually, the inevitable happened and I lost my best friend.

Luke and I stayed together, despite our general unpopularity with family and friends. Our only consolation was we were now 'official' and we could go out together whenever we wanted. We both felt guilty for hurting Maria, but Luke was such a strong character, he wouldn't let it spoil things for us. He convinced me to forget about the past and enjoy the present. Three years later, we were married.

On the surface it looked as if Luke and I had such a happy marriage, but that was only a façade. Only a few months after we tied the knot, Luke began to abuse me. This was a side of his character I'd never seen before and I tolerated it, only because I felt sorry for him because he'd recently lost his mother. But the situation didn't improve, Luke obviously was still unable to handle his grief and got into a cycle of abuse that was impossible to escape from. Every night Luke would go to the pub, drown his sorrows and then return to use me as his punchbag in a drunken rage.

I had no one to turn to. All my friends thought I was a bitch for stealing Luke from Maria; they thought I was getting the beating I deserved. The situation was getting more serious by the day and I didn't know what to do. The only person who was prepared to help me was my old friend Wayne. He listened while I poured my heart out. The amazing thing was that this was the man whose proposal of marriage I had turned down and yet he didn't once criticise me, he just listened.

Wayne didn't tell me to leave Luke, he just waited for me to fall out of love with him. He eventually convinced me I deserved better and provided me with an escape route.

Running away from Luke was just the beginning, our divorce was long and complicated and Luke succeeded in making me suffer every step of the way. Wayne provided me with a place to stay and as much emotional support as I needed. Not once did he ask for anything back. Even when the decree absolute came through, Wayne gave me enough space to regain my dignity.

It was a beautiful summer's evening and Wayne asked me if I fancied a walk out to the park. I was pleased to be asked because I was at a loose end really. As we walked through the park, the conversation turned to our schooldays and before long we were sitting on the swings recalling our funniest anecdotes. Wayne pointed out our old 'special' park bench and said, 'Come on, let's see if we can find our initials on it!' Sure enough, our teenage etchings were still visible below the latest layer of graffiti paint. 'Do you know how long it's been?' asked Wayne. I said it must have been ten years. As I turned round, Wayne went down on one knee and said, 'It's time I asked you again then.' This time I wasn't about to turn him down.

42

Pete and Sam

One Wedding and a Funeral

This story could almost be the screenplay for a Hugh Grant movie but this really happened. I was still very much in love with Jill even though we had been divorced for years. She had always called the shots in our relationship and breaking up was no exception. I'd never been able to move on because I saw my three children regularly and I would drop everything the moment Jill called if she needed help with them. When I was away from my family, I was a very lonely person; I had no social life to speak of. My heart still belonged to Jill, although I knew there was no real chance of us getting back together.

I had spent a whole year on my own because I didn't want to take any emotional baggage into my next relationship. My eldest daughter was mature enough to know what was going on and she asked me when I was going to get a new girlfriend because she was worried about me. I wasn't about to have my own daughter feeling sorry for me, so I decided to make a concerted effort to move on. I looked at my diary and surveyed my future. I noticed that the following Saturday was my friend Jim's wedding. As I thought about it, a strange comforting feeling came over me. Immediately I felt like everything was going to be all right, but I didn't know why.

For the first time in ages I felt really positive about the future. The feeling was so strong that I told everyone about it. My friends suggested that maybe I might get lucky at the wedding and one of them suggested I bought a lottery ticket just in case the feeling was about money.

The night before the wedding, my brother and I checked into a charming little hotel for the night. We were due to meet up with Jim at the pub for a good old drink with his family and friends on his last night of freedom.

To our surprise the bride popped in to say hello. Everyone was shouting, telling her to go because it was bad luck, but Sara just laughed and said she wasn't going to miss out on the fun. I remained silent throughout all of this because I was too busy staring at her bridesmaid Sam. She had the most welcoming hazel-brown eyes. That feeling I'd been having suddenly increased in intensity. This is who I was destined to meet, I concluded. Now all I had to do was make her mine. I was so dumbstruck by Sam's beauty that I couldn't move from my seat. They only stayed a few minutes because Sara wanted to get her beauty sleep before her big day. After they left, I kicked myself for not taking a chance. I knew I had to be prepared for the reception the following day, otherwise I would miss my chance to talk to Sam. I planned to watch for her going to the bar and then I would coincidentally arrive at the bar at the same time.

The other guests at my table at the reception must have thought I was very rude. I didn't have time to make polite conversation, I was too busy watching Sam and waiting for my moment. Unfortunately, I hadn't anticipated the fact that she would be waited on for most of the reception and by the evening I was getting very frustrated. But eventually I saw her make a move to the bar and I was off like a shot. As I approached her, I realised I had no idea what I was going to say to her, but it didn't seem to matter because Sam seemed to be really pleased to talk to me. It was the start of the love affair of a lifetime and I fell for her within months. I got the impression that Sam was holding something back and I began to wonder if I was scaring her away because I had kids. The worry began to eat me up inside and I couldn't bear it any more so I asked Sam to be honest with me. Sam told me the problem was she had arranged to go to Australia for six months and didn't know how to tell me.

When the dreadful day for her to leave arrived I was inconsolable. I was so upset I couldn't even take her to the airport. While she was gone I missed her terribly, but at least we could keep in touch by e-mail. It was hurting, but I was coping. Then several things happened which would change my life for ever. First, my mum was diagnosed with cancer and the prognosis was not good. I spent her final months taking her in and out of hospital and eventually we had to say goodbye. Dad always thought he would be the first to go because he was older. He couldn't take the stress and had a heart attack; fortunately he survived. But, if that wasn't enough, I was told that my daughter was ill and might have to have a colostomy bag.

I was so overwhelmed by these three disasters happening together that I couldn't cope. I ended up having a bit of a breakdown. The only person I could turn to was on the other side of the world, so I poured out my story of misery on e-mail to Sam. She was supposed to be having a good time and getting away from it all, but every time she went on line, she would have an emotional e-mail dumped on her. What was worse, was that I was so wrapped up in myself, I began to forget to ask her how her trip was going. Not surprisingly, Sam stopped reading my messages and I didn't hear from her again.

The dust began to settle and I realised that I had been really unfair to Sam. Just like that day at the wedding reception, I needed a plan to win her back. When she arrived home, the first thing she did was tell me it was all over between us, but I had been expecting that. For the last months of her holiday, I had put myself in her shoes and I knew I had a lot of work to do. I let her know that I was extremely sorry and gave her some space. Slowly, I began to show her that I wasn't the completely self-centred person who ruined her holiday, just a lonely guy who had had some bad luck. This is proving to be a lot more difficult than chatting her up at the bar, but I still have that feeling that everything is going to be all right.

43

Nickie and Wahid

There's something about Wahid . . .

By the time my friend Hilary and I arrived on our Tunisian holiday, we were exhausted. It had been a hard year at work and all we wanted to do was sit and relax and do as little as possible. There was a little nightclub next door to our hotel and before long we got into the routine of going in for a couple of *boukas* before hitting the dance floor. We were giving all men a wide berth on this holiday because we had heard plenty of stories back home about the dodgy things that went on in Tunisia.

Hilary was the first to break our 'no men' rule. She

got chatting to a guy in the club called Wahid and before long she introduced him to me. At first I thought he was some kind of nutcase but, after a couple of dances, I was rather charmed by him. Wahid seemed to know everyone in the club. He introduced Hilary to his rather sexy looking cousin and the stage was set for both of us to enjoy a holiday romance.

We had days drinking wine on the beach and dancing the night away at the club. We even got to meet Wahid's parents who seemed really nice. Wahid told me that he didn't live in Tunisia any more because he had a job at Hamburg airport.

By the time the holiday was over I was in love. Wahid had promised to call when I got home and to my surprise, he kept to his word. He informed me there was a bit of a problem because he lived in accommodation on site at the airport and that phone calls and visitors were not allowed. That meant that I would always have to wait for him to call me.

The months passed and I missed Wahid so much that I decided to go out to Germany to see him. I stayed in a hotel and he came to see me every night. We had a fantastic time, seeing the sights, eating at romantic restaurants and, of course, making love.

I was a big career girl and had no time for thoughts about marriage, but now my whole outlook on life was changing and all I wanted to do was be with Wahid. I really wanted him to come to London, but it wasn't as simple as it sounds. He needed a visa and the only way he could get one was if I invited him officially, so I sent a letter to the embassy. Wahid then went for an interview, but told me he was convinced that he was going to be turned down. I found this surprising because when I had spoken to the officials at the embassy, they had given me the impression that it was just a formality and that there would not be a problem processing the visa.

After my second visit to Germany, I discovered I was pregnant. My heart really wanted the baby, but my head told me that it wasn't possible. I had no money, and the father was in another country. I was desperate to talk to Wahid but, of course, I was unable to contact him and had to wait for what seemed like eternity for him to call me. I was expecting him to be shocked and surprised about the pregnancy because we had always been careful about contraception, but he received the big news with indifference. Why was he acting so strangely? We decided that an abortion was the only sensible way forward. My parents were very supportive and I cried throughout the whole experience. During that time, Wahid only called every couple of weeks instead of every day.

In the new year, Wahid asked me to fly out to Tunisia and visit his family with him. This time he sounded a little more normal. During my stay, he asked me to marry him. The proposal wasn't exactly the height of romance, particularly as he said we couldn't actually get married for a couple of years, but I was happy anyway. Wahid's family were extremely welcoming and I also met his elder brother's girlfriend, Lisa, who was also from London.

Not long after my return, Wahid called and said, 'If we're going to spend the rest of our lives together, there's something I must tell you, but you must come here to Germany so I can tell you face to face.' He sounded serious, but I was starting to get angry – did this guy think I was made of money? I told him I couldn't afford it but he pleaded with me. I demanded that he told me on the phone but he refused. There was obviously something strange going on and I felt that I was about to discover something I didn't want to know. I certainly wasn't going to go all the way to Germany to find out, so I decided to take a guess at it. 'You're gay, aren't you?' He denied it. 'Have you found someone else? Is there another woman?' Wahid told me to calm down and said sheepishly, 'Well there is *sort of* another woman in my life.' I couldn't bear to hear the pathetic excuse he was about to give me, so I put the phone down on him.

Having half the story turned out to be worse than knowing the whole truth. My phone kept ringing, but I let Wahid stew while I polished off a bottle of wine. Eventually the sound of ringing got on my nerves; I picked up the receiver and without even checking who it was, blurted out, 'Tell me the whole story now or I'll hang up again.' Wahid told me he was so desperate to get out of Tunisia that he had married a German girl in order to get a visa. He confessed that he lived with his wife, not at the airport. Hundreds of questions raced through my mind. How was he able to stay with me at the hotel? Why hadn't his family told me? Why had he lied to me for nine months? I shouted down the phone, 'I never want to speak to you again!' and hung up, this time removing the plug from the wall.

A rough night and one hell of a hangover later, I found myself on the phone to Lisa. I told her everything, but she told me that she already knew and that she had more details. She told me that it was true that Wahid had only married for a visa. When he got to Germany, his wife didn't help him at all and would spend most of her nights out drinking. Sometimes he would arrive home from work to find her in bed with someone else. She had demanded a baby but he refused, so she got pregnant by someone else.

At that point he had decided to go home to be with his family and think things through and that's when he first met me. Now he was in love, but in a mess. Lisa even knew about my pregnancy and told me that Wahid's wife was giving birth at about the same time as I was having an abortion. After all these revelations, I was beginning to soften up. I whipped out my credit card and booked myself on a flight to Hamburg.

Our story doesn't have a fairytale ending yet, because there's a lot more heartache to come during Wahid's divorce. But I do know that among the heap of lies I have heard over the last year there is one truth: we do love each other and we will get through this.

44

Thomas's Story

Secrets and Lies II

Over my thirty years, I had always been a bit of a 'mummy's boy'. It's embarrassing to admit that I only moved out of my mother's house when my girlfriend Jane pressurised me to move in with her. Mum and I had been close since before I could remember. My dad walked out when I was just a toddler, so I suppose it had something to do with us pulling together to get through the bad times. Mum never had any money but, through some sort of miracle, I never went short of anything I really needed. There was no doubt in my mind that she had given me the best she could and I felt indebted to her.

After I moved out, I still visited Mum every day and made sure she never needed anything. Two years ago Mum had a stroke, which left her practically unable to look after herself properly. She was so desperate to keep her independence and with it her dignity, she relied on me even more heavily. I felt obliged to help her, but it was getting to be all too much for me to handle. I was beginning to cut corners at work and my relationship with Jane was suffering. It wasn't just the number of visits I had to make. Mum started telephoning in the middle of the night, just because she heard a noise or to say she was cold because the heating wasn't working properly. I suggested that Mum let me get her some home help, but she was too proud and she wasn't having any of it. It was obvious that what Mum really wanted was me back home, but what could I do? I was grown-up now; I had my own life.

I think you really know you have grown up when you start having to take responsible decisions for your own parents. After a lot of heartache and soul-searching I decided that Mum would have to go into a retirement home. I felt so guilty, but at least I knew she would be safe in there. When I first broke the news to Mum, she was horrified and flatly refused to go. Fortunately, her GP insisted that she would be better off living somewhere where she could be kept an eye on and only then did she reluctantly agree to go.

Soon after Mum moved into the retirement home our relationship began to change. She would accuse me of not caring about her any more and she stopped phoning me altogether. We had gone from one extreme to another and it made me feel strange. It was like she was now severing all links with her own son so she could die in peace.

Now when I visited her, she became argument-ative. I thought this was just a symptom of her stroke, but then on the day she said, 'Thomas, I am finished in this place, maybe you should go and look for your real mother.' I took her words with a pinch of salt to start with and I told her to stop saying such hurtful things, but she carried on insisting that she was not my real mother. Not long after that episode, poor Mum had a heart attack and died.

Long after the funeral I remembered what she had said and I couldn't get it out of my mind. I decided to do some digging around in Mum's things and found out it was true; I was adopted soon after I was born. I can't begin to explain how I felt, I had been fed thirty years of lies and what made it worse was that we were so close; why didn't she tell me sooner?

It took me a while to come to terms with it but eventually I decided I wanted to try and find my natural mother. But where was I to look? About the only contact from the past I had was our old neighbour

Betty, so I dropped in and had a cup of tea with her. When I started asking all these questions about my childhood, she started to look decidedly uncomfortable. The more I asked, the more I sensed she was hiding something. While she was talking my eyes glanced around the room looking for anything that might give me a clue to her secrets. My gaze stopped abruptly on a picture of her children on top of the television. There was an uncanny similarity between their smiles and my own. But Betty was black and I am white, there was no way there could be a family connection here, could there? I had seen the movie *Secrets and Lies* where the black woman finds out she has a white mother. I thought it was an excellent movie, but that was fiction. The same thing couldn't be happening in my life. Just then Betty started into a long speech about how attitudes in society were different thirty years ago and I knew what was coming next. Yes, Betty is my natural mother. I didn't know what to feel, angry because I had been lied to for so long or relieved that my mother was alive.

Just like the characters in the movie, we had to spend some time adjusting and getting to know each other. I recently got engaged to my long-suffering girlfriend and we had a big party to celebrate. When the speeches came, I had no idea what I was going to say when I got on my feet, so I started to tell this one. By the end of it everyone was practically in tears.

There was only one thing left to do. I turned to my fiancée and said, 'Jane, this is my mother.' Betty's face was just full of love. Since then we have been making up for lost time. But the revelations were not over for Mum, because I have just told her she is going to be a grandmother.

45

Emma and Steve

Thelma and Louise, Eat Your Hearts Out!

My best friend Jackie and I had been fed up with our jobs for ages. On drunken nights out together we had fantasised about what it would be like just to quit our jobs and go travelling. One night we made a pact to start saving so we could make this dream a reality. Two years later we walked into our respective bosses' offices and dumped them.

After our last day at work, Jackie and I met at a bar. We toasted the end of our miserable nine-to-five lives and said goodbye to all our man troubles in London. Now we were free, we were going to spend the next six months driving across America and it seemed like our adventure was going to last a lifetime. I had no idea that it actually would.

We arrived in Boston at the start of a new chapter in our lives. For the first few days we were just like ordinary tourists, but after a while we started to blend in with the locals. Part of our master plan was to buy a second-hand car and use it to drive to the west coast stopping off along the way. The exchange rate was not as good as we had expected so we couldn't afford a really good car, but none the less we still got one. Two weeks later we drove into the sunset on what was the start of our real adventure.

Now this was just like being in the movies, radio on, the wide-open roads and the solitude. We were the English Thelma and Louise. The more off the beaten track we got, the more people were intrigued by two English girls travelling alone together. We were able to cash in on this and get the odd casual job. I think some of those people employed us just so they could listen to us talk.

One evening we were in the middle of nowhere, just waiting for the next town to appear over the horizon so that we could find a motel to rest and it seemed to be taking for ever. Suddenly, the car's engine cut out and refused to start again. We had no idea what we were going to do, there was no phone, no traffic and it was getting dark. In desperation Jackie said she thought we had just passed a house a couple of miles back, so we took the chance and went to look for it. What seemed like a couple of miles in the car seemed at least double the length on foot. Thankfully Jackie was right, there was a house. We were both very scared at this point because, in the movies, this is where a burly guy brandishing a shotgun is supposed to open the door. What we actually saw was a very well-dressed man who was drop-dead gorgeous! He smiled and introduced himself, 'Hi, I'm Steve, can I help you?' Not only did he invite us in for a rest, but he went and towed our car for us. When he got back he said, 'I'll do you a deal, I'll try and fix your car and you fix us all some dinner.' And that's just what we did.

We all ended up talking into the early hours of the morning, I just found Steve so interesting, I wanted to learn all about him. Jackie kept kicking me under the table because she thought I was being too obvious. Steve offered to put us up for the night in his house and by this time we had no choice but to accept. Just to be on the safe side, Jackie and I moved the bed against the door in case he tried to come in.

The next day just as we were leaving, I felt a wave of emotion come over me like I was leaving a true loved one behind, so I just said, 'Steve, can I call you during our travels?' He nodded in a rather cool way like you only see in Westerns and we drove off, knowing that wasn't the last we'd seen of him.

I called Steve from every town we stopped at and told him everything about our trip. He told me he didn't care what I was talking about; he just loved to hear my voice. Two months later, Steve flew out to meet us in San Francisco and we spent three weeks alone together while Jackie went off to visit some friends. Just before I flew home, Steve took me for a drive to watch the sunset. He rummaged around in his pockets for a moment and then said, 'Look, I know it's a bit early but . . ." and produced a ring! I said yes right away and set off home to England to be ridiculed by friends and family for falling in love so quickly. But over the coming year, Steve and I kept in touch and visited one another whenever we could and our wedding plans are well under way. I think my story has a better ending than Thelma and Louise's. I'm still taking 'the plunge', but unlike them, get to live happily ever after.

46

Nick and Toni

It's the Hair Wot Done It!

I will never forget the moment I met Toni. She walked into the building where I worked on her first day. Even now, many years later I can recall every detail of the way she looked. She had the most amazing hair I'd ever seen. Her locks were long, blonde, cute and curled. Her bright red suit combined with her seemingly permanent smile to leave me feeling like something special had happened to me that day.

The most important thing in my life back then was my job. I worked in a highly competitive field and nothing was going to stand in the way of me making it to the big time. My girlfriend Karen had a similar attitude towards her career. We both agreed that we didn't have time for marriage and children so it seemed we were extremely compatible.

It was the middle of the eighties property boom, and Karen and I had bought a flat together as an investment. It was hardly a convenient place to live as I had to commute nearly eighty miles to get to work, so when I was told that our company was moving even further away I had to consider alternatives. Toni lived in a big house with her brother and had once rented out her spare room to one of our colleagues, so I asked her if she would rent it to me during the week. Now instead of spending four hours or more in the car every day, I had time on my hands to socialise with my work friends and, of course, Toni. We would often find ourselves at a loose end and went out for dinners together. We got so used to living together, that Toni would sometimes knock on my bedroom door in the morning to see if I wanted any of my clothes ironing. Gossip circulated at work about our 'relationship', but at that point we were nothing more than good friends.

I had never considered that I might have romantic feelings for Toni, but now I found myself going to bed at night wondering what it would be like to be on the other side of the wall that separated our bedrooms. Once I snuck into her room while she was out, just to get closer to her. It was decorated in such a feminine way, in peaches and cream and smelled of Chanel No. 5. My fantasy became a crush, but still I did nothing.

My career progressed and I had to move away to Manchester, where I rented a house. Karen remained in our flat as her job was still nearby, and we visited each other when we could. By now we were used to living hundreds of miles apart.

I really missed Toni and to my surprise I found out that she felt the same, so I invited her to stay in Manchester for a few days. I was hardly able to sleep wondering if anything was going to happen between us. It was like being a teenager in love, but ten times as strong.

Soon afterwards, we agreed that we would meet for a drink. Those teenage 'butterflies' were back as I waited for Toni in a Soho bar. What was going to happen to us in the end? One thing I did know was I longed to be able to share my love for Toni with my friends and family. I wanted to go out and openly display my feelings for her without fear of being found out.

Later that evening Toni and I walked arm in arm along the South Bank and gazed across the Thames at the illuminated buildings of Westminster. Toni told me that she now felt completely incompatible with her new husband. 'You know, Nick, you were supposed to talk me out of getting married, but instead you just went on about my hair.' This time I wasn't going to miss my chance with Toni. Fate had provided me with enough signs and it was about time I started taking notice. Things had not been going well with Karen since we'd moved to London, and after nine years together I finally found the courage to end our relationship. It was one of the hardest things I've ever had to do.

Soon Toni and I were moving in together and attempting to make the impossible, possible. We were both aware that most affairs never last once they become official relationships, but we believed we were different. One year later we returned to that spot on the South Bank on a beautiful balmy June evening. Toni must have known what was coming as I went down on one knee and presented a bottle of chilled champagne and two glasses but, for once in my life, I was lost for words. My eyes suddenly focused on a poem that was engraved into the pavement and I read it to her before asking her to marry me. The moment was perfect. So, finally, Toni was going to be my wife and it was the start of the happiest chapter of our lives.

We were married on a boat on the River Thames two years later and now we have a little daughter who has filled our hearts with more love than we ever could have imagined.

Our happiness has hit new heights since we were married and I know that this feeling will last for the rest of our lives.

If I had my time again, we would be celebrating our

tenth anniversary by now, instead of our second. I still cringe at the thought of some of the things I said and did to Toni in those early years. I am just glad that fate didn't give up on us and that the immense power of love eventually brought us together.

47

Sarah and Nikos

Call Me Shirley Valentine

My problem is that I'm a hopeless romantic. Most people seem to get more cynical with their advancing years, but I have remained as dewy-eyed about relationships as any teenager.

I had been married to Bill for nearly twenty-five years. Our kids were grown up and living their own lives and Bill had his beloved garden. I kept a busy social diary and used to go to bingo with my friends every week. One night we were all having a moan about how boring our husbands had become when my friend Jill said, 'Have you seen that film where that woman goes off to Greece without her husband and has a bit of hanky-panky with one of the locals? We should all go and do a bit of a Shirley Valentine ourselves.' Jill was just being fatuous, but the rest of us realised she was on to something. Most of our husbands were going to be glued to the telly watching football in a few weeks' time, so we came up with the idea of having a girls' holiday in the sun.

Unlike Shirley Valentine, we actually told our other halves where we were going. My husband Bill thought it was a great idea because he wouldn't have to put up with me moaning about missing my favourite TV shows. Before we knew it we were out on shopping expeditions for swimsuits and suntan lotion. Jill confessed to me in private that the reason why she had suggested the trip was because she had found out that her husband had cheated on her and if she got a chance while she was away, she was going to get her own back. I was quite shocked because all I had in mind was a bit of a 'knees up' in the odd taverna here and there.

There was a blast of heat as we stepped through the aircraft door and Jill shouted, 'Watch out Rhodes, here we come!' I think we all sensed that this was going to be a week we would remember for a long time. Our hotel was such a wonderful place, the whitewashed walls and vines growing across the terrace creating a beautiful setting. Everything took place outdoors and at night we would dine under the stars. The whole group would get together and have a few drinks afterwards and we would listen to the live music played by the hotel's musicians. I was beginning to feel romantic already and couldn't help but notice there was a dance floor there too. One of my friends noticed my daydreaming and started to poke fun at me, 'Hey watch out girls, Sarah's going all Mills and Boony on us!' I couldn't help it, the atmosphere of the night was so appealing and I really wanted to dance. Suddenly my friends stopped their ridicule for a moment. I snapped out of my trance to see a suntanned gentleman standing before me offering me his hand for a dance. I just rose to my feet and drifted on to the dance floor with him. All my friends cheered euphorically, but I was in another world as I glided around the floor with this complete stranger. As we were dancing I felt a spark between us. Afterwards he bowed, kissed my hand and introduced himself as Nikos. By now I had come down to earth and I realised he wasn't seriously interested in me, he was just being courteous.

We were only in Rhodes for a week and the days of this wonderful holiday passed quickly. Nikos and I spent some of our days together, going for walks or lazing on the beach. At night we returned to that dance floor and danced and danced. By this time I was sure there was something between us, although nothing was said. I had already told Nikos that I had a husband back at home and he confessed he was married too. But the glances and touches just made it so obvious what he was thinking.

Our last night came all too soon. I made all the others stay up as late as possible because I didn't want to be left dancing alone with Nikos. I knew where it would all lead if we were given half the chance, so I wanted them to be my conscience for me. I was sure Jill was getting her revenge on her husband by watching me, because she had spent the whole week drinking and never made a move on any man. It was about midnight when all of the group started yawning obviously and Jill led them away leaving me alone. As she disappeared she gave me a knowing wink.

Nikos took my hand and pressed his cheek close to mine and we danced; long slow dances and so close. The band finally gave up at two in the morning and that's when Nikos kissed me. After that there was no turning back. Like I said earlier, 'We did everything outdoors in Greece!' It was the best night of my life.

Since then I've been back to Rhodes, I tried to recreate romance with my husband, but it wasn't the same. I did manage to snatch a few clandestine moments with Nikos, but it wasn't enough. I knew that I wasn't the only visitor to the island whom he'd romanced, but part of his charm was that he made me feel like I was the only one.

I want to go back again, my friends think I am off

my rocker. I have tried to forget Nikos but every time I close my eyes, I can hear the music and I want to dance with him again. I know it's foolish, but I am just scared that if I don't go, I will never have that romantic feeling ever again.

48

Janice and Alan

I'd Do Anything for a Flake

Back in the eighties, I was working for the police and was living with Ken who was also on the force. Everything was fine in our lives until Ken was attacked while on duty and was rushed to hospital. His injuries were so serious that poor Ken lost sight in one of his eyes and consequently he was forced to take disability retirement.

Ken became much harder to live with. Gone was the fun-loving and caring man I met, now he was bitter about having his life ruined by a bunch of lawless thugs and he had no one to take his frustrations out on except me. I did feel so sorry for Ken, after all, what happened was not his fault, so I tried my best to live with it.

There was quite an age difference between us. I was twenty-nine and he was thirty-seven with three teenage boys from his first marriage. We all got on like one big happy family, but my body clock was ticking and I wanted a baby of my own. Ken was dead against the idea of another child, so I put the idea to the back of my mind until he was feeling better.

One day I was at the police station and on my lunch break when I saw this guy called Alan. My friends told me they had noticed him staring at me all week. The next time I looked over in his direction, our eyes met. We both blushed like teenagers and looked away. The next thing I knew, he was leaning over my shoulder placing a Cadbury's Flake on the table in front of me and he whispered in my ear, 'Go on . . . treat yourself.' I didn't know what to say.

The next day Alan tracked me down at my desk and asked me out for a drink. I melted at the sight of his lovely brown eyes and accepted the invitation without really considering Ken's feelings. I felt extremely guilty not telling him, but I felt like I deserved a little freedom after the way he had treated me. Alan met me at the bar and when he arrived, the first thing he pulled out of his pocket was another Flake. We just laughed and in turn, it really helped my stomach butterflies to go away. Conversation flowed easily between us and we had the most fantastic evening. I felt so light, like I could fly; all my problems with Ken seemed a million miles away and I didn't want the night to end. Just before I left I had to ask one burning question, 'Alan, are you married?' Alan's silence confirmed my suspicions and I was thoroughly disappointed. We tried meeting a few more times but it was becoming more difficult to lie to Ken and I was getting too hurt. I took a step back and considered my choices. Have an affair or go back to a depressing man who wouldn't give me a baby. I decided to dump them both.

For the next four months I did a lot of crying. I missed having a man in my life but it gave me time to think about what I really wanted. I had given Alan the ultimatum of leaving his wife if he wanted to be with me and I told Ken that I was fed up with his self-pity and I was going to find someone who would give me a baby.

One night there was a knock at the door. I opened it to find Ken sporting a smile, which was something I hadn't seen in quite a while. He held up a box that looked decidedly like it was from the jeweller's. 'Janice, I've missed you so much . . . and you were right. It's time for me to get my act together and stop being so miserable. I want to start a new life and if it's a baby you want then great, let's do it . . . let's get married!' I was absolutely flabbergasted, but I didn't rush to accept. I took time to think about it long and hard before deciding to go for it.

We decided to move away to the countryside to start our new life. We sold our London flat and put the proceeds together with Ken's disability settlement to buy an old barn. We converted it into a luxury home and a small restaurant. We had a wonderful wedding and not long after I found out I was pregnant. Everything had fallen into place and I was so happy, I felt as if my life had reached its peak. But once you reach a peak, there is only one direction in which to go – down! I lost the baby in a painful miscarriage then, three years later, we lost the business and with it our home. Not surprisingly, the arguments started. Every time they happened, Ken would storm off to the pub and drink a skinful. Ken started an affair with a woman in the village, but secrets don't last long in the country and it wasn't long before I found out. We were divorced a year later.

Once again I surveyed the mess I was in. I wanted to stay in the countryside because I'd made good friends there. I found myself thinking about Alan and what might have happened if I had gone with him instead. I decided to write him a letter and bring him up to date. Obviously, I hadn't stayed in touch with him so I just mailed the letter to his old address. I had no idea if he would actually read it as it had been over five years since I'd seen him. When I didn't get a reply, I assumed he'd either moved or just wasn't interested.

Four months later on I was walking down the village high street in my wellingtons, when I heard a familiar voice shout, 'I like the boots!' I turned around to see Alan waving from his car. 'God, I missed you,' I sighed and hugged him tight. We spent the rest of the day catching up and drinking lots of wine. We had so much to say and many issues to deal with, but it was so nice to be back in Alan's company. The day turned into a weekend and the sex that should have happened all those years ago exploded between my sheets that night.

Alan told me he was still married, but assured me he really was in the process of ending it. The weekend was so passionate that I felt confident to reiterate my ultimatum from five years ago, 'Make a clean break from your wife and then you'll find there's plenty more love where that came from.' Alan agreed and I moved back to London to be closer to him.

One day Alan came round and announced, 'I've got some news for you, I've left my wife.' I wondered why he wasn't smiling. That's when he told me he'd met someone else and was moving in with her. I felt my heart being ripped open; I cried like I had never cried before. Alan patted me on the shoulder and then coldly turned, walked straight out of the door and out of my life. I never heard from him again.

So here I am, all alone. I'm now in my forties and still childless. What did I do to deserve this?

49

Mike and Suzanne

If Only They'd Invented the Internet Twenty Years Earlier

I have lived in Florida all my life and became an Anglophile at a very early age. The explanation for this lies with my next-door neighbour. During the Second World War, Jack was a Lancaster bomber pilot based in the UK and, as a child, I had heard all his adventure stories about his bombing raids over Germany and the magical time he spent in England and the warmth of the English people. He also met the love of his life there and got married.

The summer of 1979 was a summer I will never forget. Jack told me his granddaughter, who was about the same age as me, was coming over from England to visit and he asked me if I would show her around. I was only thirteen at the time, but Suzanne still touched my heart. To begin with she was so shy and barely spoke to me, but after a while she relaxed and started to come out of her shell. When she spoke it was like she was royalty or something and she was so polite all the time, it made me laugh. I proudly introduced her to all my friends and earned myself a few cool points with them. We were still kids at heart though, and we spent the summer playing together and just having fun. By the time she returned to England we were very close. I was beginning to have feelings like I'd never had before. Now she was gone, I had a sick feeling inside like someone had taken away part of my soul. I wondered what I was going to do without her.

Suzanne and I kept in touch by letter. She used to call herself my 'English Rose' and wrote all about the feelings she was discovering too. I still have a box of letters to this day. We both shared a dream that one day we would see each other again. That dream came true but we had to wait for it. Twelve years in fact.

When she walked through the gate at Orlando airport it seemed like a fairytale. Suzanne had blossomed into an extremely sophisticated-looking woman. I was so overwhelmed by her beauty I thought there was no way I would have ever approached her if I hadn't known her already. She looked so out of my league. But under that glamorous exterior, she was the same old Suzanne that I knew and loved. I had been planning our reunion for years. I took her everywhere I knew that was special to me. Places where I walked, my favourite beaches and the most romantic restaurants I could think of. It was like we had never been apart; we seemed to fit so well together. Over our last candlelit dinner before she returned, I told Suzanne not to worry because I wasn't going to wait another twelve years before seeing her again. I arranged to visit her in England a few months later.

After she went home I sent her more love letters. Back then they took nearly two weeks to be delivered and long-distance phone calls not only cost a fortune, but they were very poor quality and we would practically have to shout at each other. If only we had had the Internet back then!

I was so in love with Suzanne, just before I left for London, I bought an engagement ring. On my way to the airport, I stopped off at work to pick up my last-minute messages. My boss saw me and called me into his office. He had a particularly big message for me: I was fired! I was so shocked that I thought I'd better return the ring because I could no longer afford it. So I arrived in London jet-lagged and jobless. I couldn't help but tell Suzanne all about my story of the ring. I wish I hadn't, because I think it caused the first crack in our otherwise perfect romance.

The years went by and we darted across the Atlantic whenever we could afford it and eventually I did get Suzanne that engagement ring. We were so in love but the distance was really beginning to become a problem. I didn't want to move to the UK and Suzanne's family didn't take kindly to the idea of us living together in Florida.

I guess the end came when Suzanne was last in Florida in 1994. By now she was working for an airline, so I got to see her whenever she had their flight to Orlando or Miami. The USA was hosting the World Cup that year and on one night I had arranged to go with Suzanne and her flight crew to see a game. Suzanne barely spoke to me that night because I didn't know anything about soccer and I got the impression she was flirting with this Irish guy in the group. I got so jealous that I nearly started a fight.

The next time I called Suzanne in England, a man answered the phone and informed me that Suzanne was engaged to someone else now and she didn't want to talk to me any more. I couldn't understand why she didn't tell me herself and looking back, maybe that guy was spinning me a line so he could have Suzanne for himself. Either way, it worked and I never heard from my English Rose again.

I've never forgotten about Suzanne and sometimes I still read through her love letters, which I still keep in a special box. I found out that she's now happily married to some guy from the Midlands. I guess someone else is now wearing my engagement ring. But that's not the only thing I left in England. I left my heart there too.

50

Hayley and Martin

Would You Trust a Casanova?

I had been with my boyfriend Sam for eight years. It was one of those relationships that just ambled on and on through years of mediocrity. We never discussed marriage, probably because we both knew that our relationship wasn't going to last for ever. But time was marching on and my body clock was ticking and I was beginning to think about the possibility of children.

It was about this time when I met Sam's friend Martin. He was a bit too flash for his own good and had a bit of a reputation for womanising. Despite all that, I couldn't help but be drawn to him. My body would start to tingle any time Martin was around. I decided this was all to do with my broodiness and pushed my feelings to the back of my mind. After all, Martin was Sam's friend so there was no way either of us was going to start anything. I was wrong.

One night I was babysitting for a friend when Martin appeared at the front door. I wondered why he'd picked a night when he knew that Sam wasn't around to come and visit. I wasn't left in the dark for long because within a few minutes of his arrival Martin was telling me of his undying love for me. Even though I couldn't believe my ears, I did manage to keep my head. I remembered his reputation and I gave some consideration and thought of his poor girlfriend to whom he'd been unfaithful so many times. I took a deep breath and told Martin that I was sorry, but nothing was going to happen between us. As I spoke, my heart was just crying out to pull him close and have him right there and then.

The babysitting 'incident' was never mentioned again, but any time I saw Martin, I would feel his stare burning into me. My guilt complex became even worse when Martin's girlfriend confided one night. We were having one of those girlie chats in the women's toilets when she told me that Martin never paid her any attention despite the fact she knew he wasn't seeing anyone else. She went on to admit they hadn't had sex for two months and was beginning to think that Martin was really gay. She'd put two and two together and decided that all the philandering with so many women in his life was a sign of self-denial. While she was talking I had worked out that it was about two months since he had tried it on with me.

Christmas was coming, Sam and I were rowing as usual about whose family we were going to have Christmas dinner with. It had all got out of hand and Sam had said some very hurtful things and stormed out of the house. I was desperate for a shoulder to cry on, and guess who just happened to be available? Martin and I went for a long walk on the common and before long I'd stopped talking about Sam and moved on to telling him everything about the feelings I'd been having. Martin said nothing, then all of a sudden he stopped and pulled me towards him. I hadn't had any serious sexual contact for two years, so I was rendered powerless by Martin's manly actions. He reached inside my clothes and caressed me, sending my body into ecstasy. Now there could be no turning back. Martin laid me down in a secluded cove and we made love right there and then. The combination of the passion and the fear of being caught made it the best sexual experience I had ever had.

After our first incredible experience, Martin and I just couldn't stop. Our affair lasted an incredible nine months. One day Martin called me and said that he had something important to say to me, so I prepared myself to be dumped. But instead he revealed that he had split up with his girlfriend because he was in love with me. He promised that he was a new man and that his wandering days were now over. Naturally, he was expecting me to end my relationship with Sam, but I just couldn't stop thinking about Martin's reputation and how he could now do to me what he'd done to his girlfriend. When I told Martin that I couldn't trust him, we had a blazing row and after that I thought I would never speak to him again.

I went back to Sam and tried to pick up the pieces of our relationship. By comparison to Martin our lives were dull, but at least I could rely on Sam. I didn't think much about Martin until I received a secret birthday card from him. In it he said that he was still waiting for me and that he would do anything to earn my trust. Something told me this was the last chance I was going to get with Martin. I took one last long look at Sam and thought, is this the father of my children? and I had to conclude that he wasn't.

So, heaven help me, but I am going to take a chance with Martin. I just hope I am not jumping out of the frying pan and into the fire.

51

Michael and Liz

The smile High club

It was 19 March 1995. My life hadn't been going too well and I was flying around the USA to get away from it all. When I boarded in New York, I thought I was bound for Atlanta, but actually I was flying right into a time I would never forget.

I was one of the last passengers to board. As soon as I found my seat, a flight attendant offered me a drink. This was nothing out of the ordinary, but as soon as I finished it, she brought me another one without asking. I would have put it down to good service if it hadn't been for the extraordinarily warm smile she gave me every time we spoke. On my return flight I was looking around the cabin when there she was again, but this time she was a passenger. Upon recognising me, that familiar smile came over her face once more. She unbuckled her seat belt and moved over to the empty seat next to me and we proceeded to chat for the rest of the flight. Her name was Joan and she told me she shared an apartment in New York with another flight attendant called Liz. Joan and I got on really well so we decided to swap addresses. I put her card in my wallet and promptly forgot all about it. In New York I caught a flight to Glasgow to spend the last week of my holiday in Scotland before returning home to London.

I pushed open the door of my flat to find the usual pile of bills, junk mail and . . . a letter from New York! I was surprised that Joan had written already. She said she had some time off coming up and proposed a visit to London. We visited all the tourist sights that you never get around to doing if you live in London. We saw the Tower of London and the Crown Jewels, Madame Tussauds and even paid top price for tickets to a West End musical and I have to say we thoroughly enjoyed it. During this time we both established that we would only be friends and nothing more, but Joan kept on saying how well I would get on with her flatmate Liz. As luck would have it, Liz and her family were coming over for a holiday in Scotland soon and

Joan put me in touch with them, so I could recommend some places to go. I took my responsibilities very seriously. I wrote letters and made loads of phone calls to them, to make sure they enjoyed themselves when they arrived. They were so grateful for my help that they invited me to go on holiday with them.

When they finally arrived, I couldn't believe that Liz looked exactly like Joan had described and she was so right about our compatibility; we hit it off straight away. Liz and I spent a lot of the holiday driving in the Highlands and walking in the glens together, while her parents went off visiting castles and the like. We had all day to talk and learn more about each other and by the end of the week, we probably knew more about one another than most couples who have been dating for a year. One night we were staying in this charming little Highland village. I noticed that the skies were particularly clear and proposed that we all went for a walk. Liz's father was just getting up from his seat to join us when her mother pulled him back down rather abruptly. 'You two kids go ahead,' she said, giving me a knowing smile, 'We were going to have an early night anyway.'

A black cat followed us from the hotel to the outskirts of the village. I told Liz that maybe it would bring us good luck and we might be able to see the beauty of the northern lights. We walked and talked and completely lost track of time. Unfortunately,

Michael and Liz ♡

clouds came over and we never saw anything in the heavens, but for me the magic of the evening was still alive. I sat her down in the middle of a country road and we listened to the silence. Suddenly we found ourselves kissing and the spell of the night was complete.

In the cold light of day, we both faced up to the fact that having any kind of relationship would be difficult, but we just couldn't stop ourselves and by the end of the holiday we were in love. When we told Liz's parents, they were thrilled and her mother even started talking about arranging our wedding.

Over the coming months we accumulated massive phone bills and I spent all my money flying over to America to visit Liz. One time I went over and had to work, so I paid for tickets to fly back and forth from New York to Washington twice so I could be with her. Now that was love! As we taxied down the runway, things were about to really take off for us. I gazed at Liz who was sitting facing me in the crew seat and, as we felt the aircraft leave the ground and climb into the sky, I asked her to marry me. That put her on cloud nine for the rest of the flight.

Liz and I were married in Pittsburgh on 23 August and she is the best wife any man could ever wish for, I'm so happy.

52

Albert and Scott

All Aboard the Love Train!

My home country of Hungary is not the best place in the world to be gay, so when I got the chance to come to London I was over the moon. When I first arrived I could hardly speak any English, I had no friends and the money I did have didn't go very far, but it's amazing how quickly you learn when you have to and before long I was conversing in English and meeting new people.

It was a cold November night when I first met Michael in a bar. We got on really well and within a few weeks we became the best of friends. We would stay up until the early hours of the morning talking about our hopes and dreams. I told Michael how I longed to find a partner who wanted more than a one-night stand. I wanted someone with whom I could share my life and a friend who could make me laugh. Unfortunately, Michael wasn't going to be that person because he was straight.

Michael and I continued to be great friends. He was always after girls and we had so much fun as I worked as some sort of go-between for him. I would be the harmless gay guy who would start chatting to a beautiful woman, then I'd tell her what a good match she'd be for my friend Michael and I'd introduce them. It worked every time.

One weekend we went to Brighton to relax, soak up the sun and enjoy the atmosphere, which was great. Just before we boarded the train to return to London, I proposed that Michael should now help me to have some fun. I told him that I was going to walk through the train and sit opposite the man I found the sexiest and Martin would have to come up with a way to start up a conversation. Just as we entered the carriage, I saw him. I knew instantly that it was the man of my dreams. I made a beeline for him and nearly knocked someone to the floor in my rush to get there before anyone else. During the journey, I made it obvious that I was checking him out. After a while, I looked over at Michael and indicated that he should start talking.

'Err, excuse me, have you got the time?' he said, in a pathetic display of how to start a conversation. The man just said the time and went back to his book. I spent the rest of the journey kicking Michael to prompt him to try something else, but he thought I was just punishing him for being so bad. The train pulled into London Victoria and as soon as the doors opened, my mystery man raced off through the crowds. Michael finally came up with a suggestion, I raced after the man and said, 'Excuse me, I think you've dropped this,' and gave him the piece of paper upon which Michael had written my phone number. I turned and ran for cover as I felt my face turning cherry red from embarrassment.

Three days later a man called Scott called and said in an educated American accent, 'How was Brighton? The view from the train looked pretty good!' Not long after that he invited me out for dinner, I couldn't believe my luck.

We met in a bar in Marble Arch and went on to have a wonderful night in the West End. Over a gourmet dinner Scott told me he was from America, but was teaching in Oxford. As he spoke in his gentle but confident way, I contemplated his immense beauty. I don't know why, but for some reason I felt like I could instantly trust this man and I began to relax.

A few days later, I was in my flat watching TV when

a strong feeling came over me. I felt compelled to be near Scott right at that moment. Without thinking, I picked up the phone and poured my thoughts on to Scott's answering machine. He didn't return the call until about ten thirty because he had been teaching an evening class, but confessed he had been thinking about me too. He said, 'I know it's late but I'm not tired so come over now.' I didn't have the confidence to tell him I didn't have a car and I was afraid that if I had, he would have retracted the invitation, so I called Michael to ask if I could borrow his but he was out. I ended up getting the bus all the way to Oxford and caught a cab to Scott's place. It was two in the morning before I arrived. Fortunately Scott didn't appear to mind and we went on to enjoy a wonderful night together and I fell asleep in his arms.

I was sure I had found the man of my dreams because everything between us was perfect; actually, it was too perfect. I fell in love with Scott in no time at all. It was so quick, I had to wait a few weeks before telling Scott because I didn't want to sound like a love-sick teenager. As soon as I'd said those three little words, Scott began to change. He was behaving like he was hiding something and it was scaring me to death. I was so afraid he would turn out to be like all the others and only seeing me for sex. I could bear it no longer so I pleaded Scott to tell me what was on his mind. He eventually told me that it was that he didn't want to lead me on, as he was going back home to America at the end of term and didn't have plans to come back to England. His revelation made me sad, but at least I knew his intentions were honourable.

Over the time we had left, we tried to be practical and to cool things down. But every time we parted, we always ended up back together because we loved each other too much. In the end Scott said, 'Albert, let's quit fighting this thing, it's more powerful than the two of us.' So now I'm going to move to Boston as soon as Scott can arrange a job for me out there. In the meantime we have to make do with visiting each other when we can.

Meanwhile, Michael and I remain the best of friends. He recently married one of the women I set him up with and I was invited to be his best man. He wants Scott and me to go to San Francisco so he can return the favour. Maybe we will one day. After all, without Michael's quick thinking, I would have missed my chance to be happy for ever.

53
Craig and Jay
Too Gentle for Words

I had a pretty tough time growing up. My biological parents physically abused me from an early age, so I ended up in the care of social services and was raised by foster parents. My adult life wasn't going to be much easier because when I started to think about sexual relationships, I was only interested in men.

I left my so-called home at the age of seventeen and went out looking for the love that had been so absent from my childhood. Being gay and good looking has its disadvantages as well as the obvious advantages because, despite receiving a lot of attention in bars and clubs, most guys were only interested in one-night stands or open relationships. My past experiences left me wanting much more from a relationship than just sex. Consequently, I was never the sort of guy who slept around. I had about four relationships, the longest of which lasted a year and a half. I spent a lot of my time single and lonely. I was beginning to give up on my dream of having someone as a friend as well as a lover.

By the time I was twenty-five and had seen it all, I had become so cynical about the gay scene in clubs and bars that I hardly ever went out any more. One night I decided to go to this new piano bar in the West End. I found an empty bar stool and began to soak up the atmosphere. I couldn't help but notice this guy who looked a bit like Robbie Williams dressed up in a dinner suit. Some people would look far too overdressed in such an outfit, but his rugged appearance and firm body just made him look so cool. Before long, he noticed that I couldn't take my eyes off him and he made his way over to where I was sitting. He introduced himself politely as Jay and offered to buy me a drink. I declined because I just didn't want to go through that one-night stand thing again, not even with him. Jay's voice sounded softer than his hard man image, in fact he seemed really nice. We continued to talk, discovering that we had a lot in common. He told me he was an Eastender just like me and it seemed he had experienced a tough time growing up too, though he didn't go into much detail. As we talked I realised he was much more sensitive on the inside of his rugged looks. I asked him why he was wearing the dinner suit and he explained that he used to wear it when he was a professional boxer and never really got out of the habit. When I asked why he had given up boxing he said he didn't really want to talk about it.

Time flew by and the bar was about to close. I had missed the last tube and I didn't have enough money for a cab, so I was dreading the prospect of a long trip home on the night bus. Just then Jay offered me a lift. I thought, 'Here we go, back to his place for coffee and then he'll make a move on me.' I accepted the offer because I favoured the idea of spending the night in bed with Jay over sitting next to some drunk on the bus. But Jay completely surprised me by dropping me off home without question. He politely asked if he could see me again and I immediately agreed.

Jay and I went on some wonderful dates for about two months. So far we had only kissed and cuddled, but not once had he tried to get me into bed. I thought this was all very honourable, but was now beginning to get a bit impatient. Eventually I was desperate to show my love for him physically and had to say something. When I confronted him, Jay just said, 'I don't want that sort of relationship,' and changed the subject. After that I just put him down as a married bisexual who was frightened of going all the way. The next day Jay called and told me he couldn't see me any more. I was so shocked because we were getting on so well before I mentioned sex.

Nearly a year later a friend of mine died of Aids and I felt really bad because he died without any friends or family. I decided that I could alleviate some of my guilt by helping others in the same position. I contacted the Terrence Higgins Trust and got involved with their Buddies scheme in which you befriend people who are HIV positive. About three weeks after my interview they gave me my first address to visit. Not really knowing what to expect, I knocked on the door. Can you imagine my face when Jay opened the door? We were both dumbfounded! Was this pure coincidence or was it fate? Suddenly, it all fell into place. Jay explained that he couldn't tell me he was HIV positive because he thought I would be like so many of the other men he'd met who had just run a mile when they found out. I told Jay all about my past and my relationship fears and he began to realise that we had similar needs for different reasons. We decided to pick up where we left off, but of course were still frustrated about the sex thing.

I continued my involvement with the Terrence Higgins Trust and met some really knowledgeable people there. They gave me some expert advice on how to have a super-safe sexual relationship and we were told we should be OK as long as we followed the rules. I have to go for regular checkups and so far, so good.

Now everything is perfect. Together we have helped each other to overcome our fears and we are so much stronger as a result. Jay's health is absolutely fine because the drugs are keeping the disease under control. As for me, I'm nearly thirty years old and this is the first time in my life I have felt loved and secure.

54

Samantha and Matt

Sam's Awakening

Before Matt came along, I guess I'd never really had a serious relationship. There was something really special about the way I connected with him and it wasn't long before I fell in love. My parents had always encouraged me to save myself sexually until I met the right person. I had never been through that rebellious phase with them, so I had remained a virgin long after all my friends had thrown caution to the wind. I was so glad I had waited because my first time with Matt was such a sensual and positive experience.

Our beautiful romance blossomed over the years

and I began to feel like I could never live without Matt by my side. We had one of those relationships that everybody held up as an example of 'how things should be'. No one ever imagined that we would encounter any problems and it was assumed we would remain together for the rest of our lives. When Matt asked me to marry him, it was just another step on that inevitable path that had been carved out for us. Naturally I was over the moon about our engagement. We decided to set a date quite a long way in the future so we could save up for the deposit on a house.

We had always been seen by other people as a sensible couple and after a while we began to get bored with this. We were, after all, still young and we wondered when we were going to get the chance to have fun once we had taken on a massive mortgage. In a moment of sheer irresponsibility, we decided to blow our savings on a summer trip to Australia. I'm so glad we did, the indelible memories of our journey were a much better investment than bricks and mortar.

Living in one another's pockets for weeks on end brought about a change in me. It wasn't that we rowed all the time or anything like that. In fact we were perfect companions, it's just that by the time we returned I felt a bit different towards Matt but I couldn't put my finger on the cause.

Soon after our return, my parents told me they'd been doing some thinking of their own. They told me they were separating as I was now grown-up and there was no reason for them to still be together. The news came as a massive shock to me. I had always looked up to my parents and I aspired to making my marriage as successful as theirs.

So my mum and dad's perfect relationship was a sham. The revelation left me feeling lonely and vulnerable even though Matt was there for me every step of the way. I suppose I felt like I had been cheated.

I began to analyse my relationship with Matt and realised that I had put all my emotional eggs into one basket. For the past few years, Matt and I had spent every waking hour with each other and I had totally neglected all my friends. I decided to change my ways and set more time aside for my friends.

On the first girls' night out, I realised just how much I missed them. The more time I spent with my friends, the more it seemed to make me restless in my relationship with Matt. We tried taking the odd week off, but we never stuck to it and would always end up seeing each other before the time was up. I still felt uncertain about our relationship, but put it down to 'going though a funny phase'. I thought I would get over it, but I didn't.

Eventually, I had to do something, so I took the plunge and arranged to meet Matt in a pub. I told him that I still loved him, but the engagement was off until I had sorted my feelings out and would it be OK if we were just friends for a while. Matt couldn't hold back his emotions and he wept openly. After that he didn't say very much; he was looking for an explanation. He probably wanted me to tell him that there was another man, but there wasn't, it was just deeper than that. Earlier that evening, I had packed all Matt's belongings that were still at my place and left them just inside the door. I asked him to come back and pick them up. He seemed pretty cool about that, but as soon as we walked into the car park, he ran to his car and skidded off. By the time I got to my flat, Matt had picked up his things, left his key behind and vanished. At that point I knew I had hurt him so much that I could never change things back.

After that day I never saw Matt again. I still don't know if I had a lucky escape or if I lost the love of my life. Maybe I'll never know, but I do hope that Matt will be able to forgive me one day.

55

Anthony and Fabiola

Two Wrongs Can Make a Right

To say I was going through a rough patch in my life was an understatement. I had been made redundant and was finding it very hard to get a new job. If that wasn't bad enough, I had just had the ugliest break-up with my girlfriend.

My friends were really good about it all, they took me out and tried to cheer me up. They all bought me drinks and assured me that this was all a passing phase. My friend Neil had a birthday party coming up and he insisted that I went along. I wasn't that keen on going because I was still depressed and I was sure going to his party wasn't going to help. I kept thinking about how bad I was going to feel when people asked me the inevitable party question, 'What do you do for a living?'

I dragged myself along because I felt like I owed Neil some support after all his kindness during my hour of need. Actually, it turned out to be a pretty good party. I met a few people I hadn't seen in a while and one of them introduced me to this girl called Fabiola. She seemed very nice, but nothing more than that at first. Unlike anyone else at the party, she seemed to take a special interest in me. She made me feel at ease, so I found myself apologising for appearing to be so down. She listened politely while I explained the situation and she was very understanding. We must have been talking for over an hour when suddenly this seriously hard-looking guy called her angrily from across the room and pointed abruptly at his watch. Fabiola's face took on a very different look, gone was the sweet caring look, now she seemed scared. 'I have to go,' she said and hurried away. I assumed the hard-looking guy was her boyfriend and that he hadn't been too pleased about the amount of time she had spent talking to me. That gave me a bit of a boost, at least I wasn't redundant with the girls.

It seemed that was the first and last I'd seen of Fabiola. I returned to contemplating my miserable life. A couple of weeks later, I was in the pub as usual when I heard friends talking about Fabiola. I probably wouldn't have overheard had she not had such a distinctive name, but, as I eavesdropped further, I heard them say, 'It's such a shame' and 'Why did she do it?' I asked them what they were talking about and they said that Fabiola was in hospital because she had tried to kill herself. I couldn't believe it, she had seemed so together when I met her at the party.

I rushed to the hospital to see how she was. I arrived on the ward to find her lying in a bed all by herself. I remembered that she had no family to speak of so she was unlikely to get many visitors. Poor Fabiola didn't look very well at all, but she put on a brave face and thanked me for coming.

Of course being unemployed, I had lots of time on my hands so I just stayed there with her until the nurses threw me out. I didn't pressurise her into telling me why she had tried to kill herself, I thought she would tell me if and when she was ready. A couple of days later, she explained that she had found out that her boyfriend had been cheating on her and when she confronted him about it he had just beaten her up. This situation was happening at about the time I met her at the party, so it's no wonder she looked so frightened when her boyfriend shouted at her.

I sensed a strong protective feeling towards Fabiola and promised her that I wasn't going to let her boyfriend anywhere near her in the future. It was only then that I realised that I'd fallen for her. I also hadn't noticed that helping Fabiola had lifted my depression. At the next job interview I attended, I was offered the job and after that I never looked back. Fabiola and I have gone from strength to strength and we are both extremely happy. It's amazing how much can be achieved when two unlucky people help each other out. In our case 'two wrongs did make a right'.

56

Alison's Story

Alison's search for a Hero

When I left school, I was lucky enough to be offered an interview with a big local company within weeks of finishing my exams. At the interview, I got talking to another candidate – a guy called Stuart. We both managed to calm one another's nerves and it must have worked because we both got taken on.

Stuart and I would always say hello if we saw each other around the office and after a while we became good friends. We even went out on a few casual dates, but neither of us took it too seriously because we were still young. It was so easy for us to be together. Both of our families approved of our relationship and all of our friends thought we were good together. I had probably found my perfect match and was on the way to long-lasting happiness. The thing was, back then I didn't know it.

Come February 1987, things weren't so easy. Stuart's father had died suddenly and everyone was totally devastated and shocked. The worst thing was that he was alone when he had a sudden heart attack and he hadn't been found until the next day. I tried my best to be supportive to poor Stuart and slowly but surely he made some progress with his grieving.

Next came Easter and a little thing happened that made me think something was up. Stuart had always bought me a lovely chocolate egg and this year he forgot. I didn't worry too much and put it down to his grieving. But then one day I was taken aside at work and told that Stuart had been seeing another girl. I couldn't believe it and stormed around to Stuart's desk to demand an explanation. Stuart confessed on the spot and all too suddenly our cosy relationship was over.

I had to forgive Stuart. We still had to work together and I didn't want to have to put up with the pain every time I saw him, besides there were plenty more fish in the sea. Six months later, Stuart married his new girlfriend and I wasn't the only one who was surprised at their speed. Plenty of people told them not to rush into it, but they didn't listen. I heard that colleagues from the office were taking bets on how long they would last. Within a year they had separated, then finally divorced.

I had a few dalliances with men over the coming years, but nothing too serious. I'd thrown myself into work and earned enough money to buy myself a horse. Riding was the perfect hobby for me because it gave me a great release from all the tensions of work.

In the summer, I was invited to a friend's wedding, which was to take place out of town. I was trying to work out how I was going to get out there when Stuart popped up from nowhere holding a similar invitation. He suggested that I should go with him in his car so we could 'catch up on old times'. By now I was over him so I decided to accept.

The wedding was lovely and we both had a fantastic time. Stuart and I barely spoke to each other because we were too busy talking to all the other guests we knew. We drove home at about midnight and that's when we started to really talk. Things were getting interesting by the time we got to my place so I invited him in. Stuart was being very honest and I sensed we were now more compatible than ever, probably because we were older and wiser. That's when he dropped the big one: he admitted that his father's death had clouded his judgement and dumping me and his successive marriage were 'the biggest mistakes' he'd ever made. I could feel a renewed and stronger passion growing for Stuart, so I took the plunge for a second time.

It was so nice having Stuart back as my boyfriend, the familiarity was so comforting. My mum was over the moon and drove me mad talking about weddings before we'd had a handful of dates! This time it was deeper, more serious than before and it all happened really fast.

One weekend we were planning a romantic meal together; I was going to cook the best meal he'd ever had and who knows what was going to happen in the bedroom afterwards. I went out horse riding to clear my head, but I must have been in a daze because I got myself into a silly situation and ended up having a fall.

While I was lying in hospital I was thinking, 'At least Stuart will be here soon to sooth my bruises and my battered ego!' How wrong I was! He never arrived to visit me and it transpired that while I was in a hospital bed, he was in bed with someone else. He'd used me as a stopgap while he tried for someone else. When he got his chance with her, he dropped me like a hot potato.

I couldn't understand why in my younger years I had found love so easily and now it was so complicated. It wasn't long before I received a bouquet of flowers from a secret admirer in the office. I found out this was a man called Matt. He seemed very nice but I told him

I wasn't interested, as I had just come out of a relationship. But he wouldn't take no for an answer and it got to the stage when I had a police escort to work. Fortunately, my employers took me seriously, they cautioned him for sexual harassment and transferred him up north.

Surely my run of bad luck was now over and my knight in shining armour would now come to rescue me. It wasn't Lee, he was another philanderer and, just like Stuart, he broke my heart. I decided to give up on men and went back to my riding, the only thing I loved that I could trust.

And that's how I stayed until eighteen months ago when I met Tony. So much of us is so right, but he is scared of commitment and doesn't even want to be known as my boyfriend, even though we sleep together on a regular basis. I have got a lot of time for Tony, but he leaves me with a sense of wanting more. I guess what I'm saying is I'm not truly in love with him.

Am I expecting too much from love? Maybe this is as good as it gets and I should give up on finding my soul mate and settle down with Tony. But I can't help feeling that my knight in shining armour is out there. Perhaps he's just been a bit delayed because he fell off his horse too!

57

Debbie and Alan

Debbie's Soul Mate

I had just turned thirty when I met Alan. At the time I was desperately unhappy with my boyfriend. Alan and I got talking, not only because we worked together, but he was also in a similar situation to me in his marriage. We would meet after work for coffee and talk and talk. Not just about our doomed relationships, we also shared a passion for journalism. The more we worked together, the closer our friendship became.

I remember thinking how wise Alan was compared to my boyfriend. He made me laugh and he flattered me with his compliments about my work. I was falling for Alan despite the fact he was twelve years my senior. It wasn't long before the passion took over and we got physical. I had to end my relationship and I expected Alan to get a divorce, but his attitude was a little more old-fashioned and he told me that he thought he owed his marriage just one more try first. Thankfully for me, it didn't work out and finally we were together.

The coming year was difficult, as we were both very ambitious. It was my goal to become a magazine editor and knowing that Alan believed I could do it helped me make my dream become a reality. Unfortunately, I had to move away for my editor's job and now we could only see each other at weekends. If that wasn't hard enough, we had the emotional stress of Alan going through his divorce too.

Eventually Alan got a job near me and we moved in together. I now had everything I wanted in life. There was one problem though and that was Alan's health. I had always known he had heart trouble and needed to take some pretty strong drugs to enable him to lead a normal life. Come autumn 1997 the drugs were becoming ineffective and Alan was getting weaker. Six months later he got sacked because of his failing health. He was now waiting for a double heart bypass and valve replacement. Would you believe he had to go through this massive operation for a second time when the valve replacement didn't work?

Alan's recovery took a very long time. During that time I was so lonely I cried myself to sleep almost every night, but eventually he came home and we started to rebuild our lives.

In late 1999 the final block to our happiness was removed when Alan's divorce became final and we set the date for our wedding. On Valentine's Day next year, Alan had to fly to Belfast on business. He arrived home with a migraine headache. I gave him some hefty painkillers and we had an early night. As we snuggled close, he told me how much he loved me.

The next thing I knew it was five thirty in the morning. Alan wasn't in bed next to me but I could hear a snoring noise coming from downstairs. I assumed he'd got up to make a cup of tea or something and had fallen asleep on the sofa, so rolled over and went back to sleep. What I did not know was that poor Alan was suffering a massive brain haemorrhage and the sounds were his gasps for breath. By three o'clock the following afternoon, I was giving instructions at the hospital for his life-support machine to be switched off. My love was gone.

Being a journalist, I have a healthy scepticism for most things and the spirit world is no exception. But I have to report that when I walked down the aisle at Alan's funeral to read the eulogy, I felt a warm hand around my waist, which gave me the strength to speak without crying. It wasn't a relative or friends, as they were all at least six feet away, so maybe, just maybe, it was Alan saying goodbye.

The saddest thing about losing Alan, is that I never got to say goodbye. I miss him constantly, but I do know he wouldn't want me to spend the rest of my life feeling down. So my love, my dear Alan, I promise you I will get better.

58

Ken and Sara

shakespeare in suburbia

I had been on my own for two years following the break-up of my marriage. Finally I had the confidence to get out of the house a bit more often. I joined a sports club because I thought it might be a way to meet up with new people and before long I had a new circle of friends.

The first time I saw Sara, I felt a surge of passion inside like I had never felt before. I managed to find an excuse to talk to her because she was arranging sponsorship for the club's charity night and I gave her a particularly big donation. My intentions were all quite innocent at first, but it wasn't long before we were having private conversations about intimate subjects. Sara told me that she was very unhappily married but had a four-year-old son whom she thought the world of. She confessed she hadn't had sex with her husband since Stephen was born and now they even slept in separate bedrooms.

Sara and I became closer and closer as friends, but I didn't tell her about my romantic feelings towards her for fear of spoiling a perfectly good relationship. But one day, I'd had a particularly bad day at work and I was feeling vulnerable. Sara was so understanding that I could hold back no more and it all came flooding out. Before you knew it we were in her car having sex like a couple of lovesick teenagers. After that there was no stopping us, we took every moment we could to sneak off somewhere and make love. It wasn't long before our feelings became involved, but we were in too deep to do anything about it.

By now, it was nearly Christmas and someone decided to give us a special present that year by writing to Sara's husband to tell him all about our affair. Sara was so worried she might lose custody of her son, that she said she was going to give her marriage another go. But within a few days, she was back on the telephone. She described how she would look out to see me driving home from her bedroom balcony every day. I used to say it was just like *Romeo and Juliet*.

Three weeks later Sara arrived at my house with her belongings stuffed into a suitcase. The only thing was, she left without little Stephen. Sara was such a caring mother, she said she couldn't put him through all the upheaval of moving house. Instead she went back to visit him whenever she could and brought him to my house to visit from time to time.

It seemed nothing could stop us now and everything was going great, the sex was the best ever for both of us and we discovered feelings we never knew existed. In July we went on holiday to Spain and had a wonderful time. By the second week of the holiday Sara's eyes started to look empty. In my heart I knew she was missing little Stephen, but didn't say anything for fear of making her feel worse. After all, this was the first time they had been apart for so long.

The day after we returned home, Sara went off to see Stephen and told me not to worry about what time she came back. I could see in her eyes that she was never coming back.

Unfortunately, I was right. Sara is back with her husband who doesn't love her, the man who treats her like his housekeeper. He has even banned Sara from contacting me, so we're back to the *Romeo and Juliet* style 'drive-bys' again.

I believe everyone deserves a happy life and Sara is no exception. I understand she wants to be with her son, but why does she have to hurt herself in the process? I wish she would bring little Stephen, bring him now, so that we can all be happy together.

59

Angela and Danny

Family Misfortunes

Ten years ago I was out with my friends doing the usual Saturday night thing. We were 'on the pull' at a nightclub. On this particular night we hooked up with three soldiers who were home on leave. Normally it was me who got the ugly one because my friends were so gorgeous looking, but this time it was me who got the best-looking one. His name was Danny and we got on so well that by the end of the night I gave him my phone number. I never really expected him to call because the men you really want to see again never do, that's just the way it is.

But the next day Danny was on the phone arranging a date, I couldn't believe my luck. A whirlwind romance followed, which was so intense both of our families told us to slow down or we would burn out but we couldn't help it. Within three weeks Danny asked me to marry him.

When Danny was away with the army, he wrote every day. One Saturday morning I was really missing him when suddenly he phoned me. He said he could only talk for a moment and wasn't going to be able to write or phone again for the next few days because he was going away on manoeuvres. He said he'd sent me a special present over to his parents' house to make up for it and I should go over right away to pick it up. I rushed over to find out what it was. Danny's mum and dad made me put on a blindfold and there was some shuffling around before they said I could take it off. There before me was . . . Danny smiling from ear to ear! I was so excited I just leapt into his arms.

Over the coming months Danny and I spent every spare minute with each other. By now I was dying to have sex with him, but I was still a virgin. When I told Danny, he said it would be really nice to wait until after we were married. I thought that sounded a bit old-fashioned for a young army lad, but respected his wishes.

We had been seeing each other for a year when Danny decided he was coming out of the army because he couldn't stand being away from me any more.

One night I took a night off from Danny and went out for a few drinks with my sister with the full intention of going on to a club afterwards. But the booze just got me all horny and so I decided I was going over to Danny's to seduce him once and for all. When I arrived, his mother said he'd gone to bed early but didn't mind if I went up to his bedroom to surprise him. As I climbed the stairs, my heart began to pound with the anticipation of the passion that was about to unfold in his bedroom. I was ready! Married or not. I opened the bedroom door and slowly my eyes focused in the darkened room. As the images became clearer it was apparent that Danny was not alone in his bed. I let out a shriek of horror, which startled the bed's occupants into consciousness. Danny's face said it all, but the worst was yet to come, because he'd been sharing his bed with his sister! I just ran out of the house thinking, 'I am engaged to a pervert!' Danny ran after me and eventually caught up. He explained that Tina had just come in drunk and fallen asleep in his bed by mistake. Nothing had happened; it was the only time it had ever happened. I didn't know what to think, I needed some space. I told Danny not to call me, but over the next few weeks he begged me to come back, saying it had all been a big misunderstanding. Eventually I could stand it no more, I went back to him and we made love for the first time ever. It was a wonderful first experience and I was happy again.

Six months went by and the wedding was getting closer. One day my sister said that she'd seen Tina and Danny in the high street together and Tina looked really upset. The next thing I knew, Danny's mother was telling me that Tina was pregnant and had refused to name the father. I thought, well that must mean she's got a boyfriend and maybe now she'll leave my Danny alone in future.

Two weeks before the wedding, Tina came to see me. She sat me down and told me to prepare myself for a shock and proceeded to tell me that Danny was the father of her baby. I was nearly sick from disgust and demanded to see Danny immediately. He came round and made things worse by not denying it straight away. He confessed that Tina had a habit of coming into his bedroom and on the night in question they were both drunk and he was almost sure nothing had happened but he couldn't remember. I had no choice but to call the wedding off. The worst thing was I couldn't tell anyone why and it just destroyed me.

Danny and I went our separate ways and over the coming years we found new partners, got married and had children but I never really loved my husband the way I loved Danny.

I was at the supermarket one day when I bumped into Tina with child in tow. I was immediately suspicious because there's no way an incestuous pregnancy would have been allowed to go to full term.

When I confronted her, she admitted that she had wanted me out of Danny's life and had lied about the whole thing.

I had to get back in touch with Danny if only to apologise. It wasn't long before I managed to track him down and discovered his marriage was about as lacklustre as mine and it wasn't long before an affair started between us.

I had lots of thinking to do because there was the welfare of the kids to consider as well as my feelings. I was really in turmoil because I loved Danny so much but I was afraid that my husband would fight me for custody of the kids if I tried to leave.

My husband Chris had been really moody for some time, I had put it down to the fact we hadn't had sex in a while because I was thinking of Danny. One day Chris came home from work and told me that we needed to talk, as he couldn't go on like this any more. When I asked him what he meant, he said he had found someone else and that he didn't love me any more and wanted to be with her. He confessed he had felt that way for quite some time and had been trying to pluck up the courage to tell me. Now it was my turn. I told him all about Danny and how I had been con-templating leaving and my concerns about what he might do to the kids. Chris smiled as if a great weight had been lifted from his shoulders. He assured me that he would never try to take the children away as long as he was allowed as much access to them as he wanted. I couldn't believe it. This really was a dream come true. Chris left that night and moved in with his new love and Danny came to live with me as soon as the kids had given him the seal of approval.

I am now so happy I want to shout it from the rooftops. I feel so lucky because it's not everyone who gets a second chance like this.

60

Sarah and Sean

I Just Can't Put Him Down

My story starts a very long time ago. I was married with two small children and only twenty years old. Mark and I had been together for three years and he had turned violent on me. I wasn't the sort of person to tolerate abuse, so I left.

I was reluctant to make too much commitment to relationships with men after that. I was scared to let anyone too close in case they became like Mark. But I had youth on my side, so I gave myself time to lick my wounds and get over it all. I spent the next five years concentrating on bringing up my two boys. Then I was fortunate enough to meet someone who earned my trust. Alan was prepared to take things as slowly as I wanted to go. We lived together for four years before getting married and during that time I had two more children. I know that Alan loves me very much, we have a beautiful home and all our kids love us very much. You could say I have everything, but the problem is I am not sure if I am really in love with Alan.

A couple of years ago, I started doing a bit of part-time work. It was great and I made lots of new friends, both female and male. Basically I have always been a flirt, but I never dreamed of taking anything further than that. Until one day, when I was sitting in the canteen at work and this man came and sat next to me. I felt all my energy sapped out of my body. I felt compelled to say something and within minutes we were chatting like old friends. He told me his name was Sean and had been married for twenty-four years but was now getting divorced. I told him that I had been through all of that too, but was now happily remarried. He said, 'Oh really? I wish I had met you before you did that.' By now he was looking deep into my eyes and I was hypnotised. I felt awkward because I knew the security of my home life was being threatened by this man's very presence and I knew that having anything to do with Sean would mean trouble. After our electric first meeting, we would see each other around work and have the occasional chat.

It was pouring with rain at the end of my next shift. Sean seemed to appear from nowhere and offered me a lift home. I knew it was a mistake from the moment I slammed the car door shut. When we got to my house, I just ran inside not even saying thank you. Not surprisingly, Sean didn't talk to me for a while after that. The next time was when he told me he was leaving work. When he broke the news, I could see him searching my face for some kind of show of emotion. I tried my best to play it cool, but inside I was so shocked.

On Sean's last day I was sure he wouldn't even bother to say goodbye but he came over and apologised for avoiding me, admitting he had done this quite deliberately. He said, 'We both know how we feel and I don't want to break up any marriages, but if you want to meet up from time to time – it's up to you.' I knew exactly what he meant by 'from time to time'. He meant for sex. I told him I didn't think it was a good idea, but he gave his phone number anyway and then kissed me goodbye – I just melted.

I tried to forget about Sean, I tried to throw away his number. In the end I was too weak and I gave him a call. I had been holding back my passion for seven months now and, on my second meeting with Sean, I could take no more. I took him to bed and gave him a full demonstration of what I'd been feeling about him. It was like a bomb going off. I knew that any mixing of our chemistry would be dangerous and I was right.

Over the next four months, once a week I tried to get the sex out of my system, but I just kept filling up with more passion. Gradually, the guilt began to build up. Thoughts of my responsibilities to my kids kept entering my head and I knew I had to stop this affair. So Sean and I said goodbye. We both choked back the tears and got on with our lives.

Another four months went by and not a day passed when I didn't think of him. I would rerun all the sexy things we had done together in my mind and I would ache. I was at work one day thinking about Sean again, when I looked up and there he was standing right in front of me. He asked me back to his place for lunch and I accepted. What did we have? Each other, of course, and off we went again.

Since then, I've tried to end this affair so many times, but we just keep slipping back. I never tell Sean that I love him because I suspect he doesn't want to hear the truth and I never talk to him about my family because it makes him feel guilty. I don't know what I'm going to do because it's only a matter of time before I get found out and then it's possible that I could end up with no one. I am so grateful to my husband for providing the family with a loving environment in which to live, but I have discovered that I need more than that and it's only Sean who can provide that kind of love.